HENRIK IBSEN, 1828-1906

PEER
GYNT

A DRAMATIC POEM IN FIVE ACTS

A NEW TRANSLATION BY
HORACE MAYNARD FINNEY, M.D.

PHILOSOPHICAL LIBRARY
New York

Copyright 1955 by Philosophical Library, Inc.
15 East 40th Street, New York 16, N. Y.

55 - 13634

Set in Times Roman at the
Polyglot Press, New York City.
Printed in the United States of America.

PREFACE

> "There are a hundred faults in this thing,
> and a hundred things might be said to
> prove them beauties."
> Oliver Goldsmith: *Vicar of Wakefield.*

I

There is really nothing else like "Peer Gynt." It is perhaps the most original conception in the world of dramatic poetry. Here Ibsen has exercised powers apparently different, even in kind, different from those of any other playwright, different indeed from those he has displayed in others of his own plays.

The centering of the action in one person largely accounts for the popularity of this play. Peer Gynt's character is the key of the dramatic structure of the play. He is the all-in-all of every scene. The entire action springs from the hero at its source but finds in him its end—he dissolves himself by means of others.

Critics have often entertained themselves with speculation on the specific moral purpose of the play. A work of art must needs be moral, because it must be true to Nature, otherwise it is at strife with itself. As to the moral temper of "Peer Gynt," critics differ widely. Some regard the play as teaching the most comprehensive humanity, the story of a lost soul; others, as a caricature of the bigotry and frailties of the Norwegian people.

Such differences of view may be taken as an argument for Ibsen's candor and evenhandedness. In this play Ibsen ordered things mainly with the view to dramatic effect. He did not allow himself to be swayed from the right measures and proportions of his art.

Into the fiber of the drama Ibsen weaves home-grown, popular folk-lore, rustic sports, studied rural pastures and satire, together with something of his own childhood. John Gynt is

iii

his own father, who squandered the family fortune, and Ase
is his own mother. Ibsen has presented Peer Gynt in a full-
length portrait. He moves by fits and starts, because the
tempering and moderating power of judgment is lacking. A
thought strikes him and whirls him far off to the right, another idea strikes him and whirls him off to the left; and so
he goes vacillating and meandering hither and thither, mainly
the result of his wild and unrestrained youth.

Peer has lost his self-restraint, and he puts pleasure before
duty, making reason wait on passion. Everything about him is
shadowy: he lives in a phantom world, a daydreamer who
cannot tell fancy from fact. He argues and quotes from trite,
proverbial sayings, which relieve him of the necessity of
thinking for himself. Hence his thoughts present a strange
melody of sense and nonsense, and we often have a gem of
thought or a beautiful image followed by childish chatter. In
short, Peer by turns is lofty and ignoble, pious and profane,
bold and brazen. He grapples with no problems but hedges
them, never burns his bridges behind him but always by-passes
them, goes "roundabout." He has in him no milk of human
kindness, no regard for kindred or posterity. His religion is
sordid and superstitious, for his deep-rooted selfishness betrays
a cynical indifference. He owes no fellowship to anyone; he is
HIMSELF alone.

When he tries the supernatural, he finds that it means nothing more than the transmogrifying of squalid realities by lies
and pretenses. He is a trifler when Fortune smiles, a whimperer
when she frowns. Adversity melts his spirit to a sentimental
pulp. He is so steeped in mere sentiment that even sorrow
makes a luxury of itself—he mulls over his misfortunes, hugs
them, nurses them, buries himself in them, as if the agony
were a haven from the stings of reproach; and then he becomes
a moralizing dreamer, building castles in Spain, brooding over
past paternal grandeur, and ever reading man through the
medium of his own dreams and ambitions.

Ase's character is one of the most wonderful strokes of
human imagination. In her is a nameless something that
haunts the mind with a sense of sorrow and pity. She has a
certain domestic feminity about her, a maternal tenderness

rendered stoic by misfortune, by the fickleness of her neighbors, by the recklessness of her lackadaisical son. Always she has strength, the steadiness to carry on; through all her hardship, she preserves her tenacious spirit.

Ase's character is mirrored in the highest realms of poetry in the first three acts. Bit by bit Ibsen builds her personality. The dreams and the likes and dislikes of mother and son are the core of the play, but Ase's thoughts are ever for her boy. She will abuse him, beat him, call him a liar, yet rejoice in his fancies and prowess; now crying, now scolding.

When Peer abducts Ingrid and clambers up the hillside, Ase shakes her fist at him and hopes he will break his neck, and in the same breath she cries out: "Watch your footing!" She commands our sympathy always, for her thoughts are our thoughts.

Solveig is the beauty of the play, as Ase is its strength. Solveig is more lyric—she is poetry itself; Ase is more dramatic.

Peer meets Solveig for the first time at the wedding when she beams upon him like a revelation of purity and charm. Perhaps Solveig does not touch our imagination as enchantingly as Ase, yet she kindles a deep and homely affection in everyone that meets her, for she is steadfast and unchanged as truth itself.

In her old age, in her blindness, Solveig presents the grace and grandeur with the habits of a recluse, delineated with a beautiful consistency. In the silence and solitude of her woodland cell, there has grown up in her mind a depth of religious feeling; but in her hermitage she bears no malice, only faith and hope and charity.

After the parting of Solveig and Peer in the third act, we see less of her. In the fourth act, Ibsen briefly whisks us away to hear her homecoming song. Like the breath of an unplucked rosebud breathes Solveig's Song, as she sits singing and spinning in the sunshine by the door of her hut.

With that the curtain comes slowly down on the scene, and we see Solveig no more until the last act, where her Cradle Song becomes the grand finale of the play. We see her dressed for Whitsun services, Bible in one hand, a staff in the other, coming through the door to greet the penitent Peer, while the sun rises over the hillside, reflected in all its simplicity, in Grieg's divine tone poem.

II

The poet and the painter in "Peer Gynt" are skillfully played off, one against the other. Like Macbeth, much of "Peer Gynt" is lost in presentation, much of the wild scenery has evaporated from the stage—the landscape, the sea, the desert —and all we see on the stage is in the foreground. "Peer Gynt" with its 39 scenes, is at its best a reading play only, like "Lear." Technicolor and CinemaScope might bring out the airy, eerie background of this play and bring to life its fantasy.

Nowhere, not even in Shakespeare, is there introduced into the play so much pastoral simplicity and vernal beauty. In "Peer Gynt" the dramatic, the picturesque and the grotesque are blended with the greatest art, and the reader's mind is kindled to an almost preternatural activity. Often a mere word, an epithet, a stage direction, paints a whole scene that haunts the imagination with the air of reality, while in the midst of the scene we meet with careless and natural disgressions—with Peer soliloquizing more often than Hamlet and quoting more biblical lore than Falstaff.

The finest things in "Peer Gynt," for sheer beauty and the colors he paints, ever wet with the master's brush, are:

ACT I—Ase marooned on the roof of the old mill shed; Wedding scene at Hegstad; Surefooted Peer scaling the rocky hillside with Ingrid on his shoulders.

ACT II—Renunciation of Ingrid; The woodland background of the Saeter Girls' Dance silhouetted against the cold and solemn beauty of the cloud-capped towers of the Norwegian mountains; Peer meets the Woman in Green, the Troll Queen, and rides off to the Hall of the Mountain King on her porker; The encounter with the Boyg.

ACT III—Deep in the Pine Woods; The reunion with Solveig, the ride to the Soria Moria Castle, and the death of Ase, described with the truest touches of tenderness and pathos.

ACT IV—In this afterthought of Ibsen there is a throng of characters. Though they jostle one another, they raise and carry on the imagination that is metaphysically profound. The Sunrise at the Sphinx with the spires and minarets of Cairo in the background. The Sphinx, like the Boyg, is unrivaled for its massiveness and its eerie shadows.

ACT V opens with a glorious view of the Norwegian mountain coast as seen from shipboard, followed by one of the finest shipwrecks in all dramatic poetry. The Auction at Hegstad, Whitsun Eve in the heart of the forest, Peer groveling for leeks like old Timon of Athens, making a swanlike end, fading in music.

III

For this compound of highly colored romantic and picturesque adventure, Edvard Grieg* wrote the music. With the advent of the phonograph and the radio, "Peer Gynt" has become more popular than ever. Hardly a week goes by when one doesn't hear some "Peer Gynt" selection. Much of the play's success is due to Grieg's inimitable music, for people are ever anxious to know Ase and Solveig and Ingrid more intimately.

Like Ibsen's verse Grieg's music is characteristically Norwegian: the moment you hear his naive and plaintive melodies, you recognize the land of the midnight sun, the opal-colored morn, and the odor of the pine woods in every bar.

The Wedding begins with the scolding scene between Ase and Peer. Now Solveig appears in all her simplicity, followed by the Halling Fling and the Spring Dance, the Wedding scene and the Bridal procession. The second act opens with the Abduction of the Bride and Ingrid's Lament—a fine-wrought elegy. This is followed by the Saeter Girls' scene, against a background majestic in scope, ending in a wild, devilish and sensual song and dance. The Woman in Green and Peer riding off on her porker are dismissed with a few deft strokes. In the Hall of the Mountain King is one of Grieg's finest creations,

---

*Of the 22 Peer Gynt selections, 8 are on Peer Gynt Suites I & II, (most all records), 13 on a new Mercury LP which gives the original stage version.

and the Dance of the Dovrë King's daughter is a rich and
grotesque parody. Peer Gynt chased by the Trolls ends with
the ringing of the church bells and the flight of the Trolls. The
act closes with Peer's encounter with the Boyg; this, too, ends
with the distant sound of bells and organ from the little
church in the vale.

Deep in the Pine-Woods opens the third act. It is followed
by the Death of Ase, one of Grieg's most inspired poems.
Slowly her life flames up and dies down, repeated twice—then
a long, deep breath, and then the care is over.

The fourth act opens with the Morning Mood, one of
Grieg's masterpieces, followed by the scene between the Thief
and the Fence, set in a miniature operatic scene for two
voices. In the Arabian Dance, Oriental and sprightly in character, the whole becomes a graceful ballet, with a song and
dance by Anitra in the interlude. Peer Gynt's Serenade closes
the Oriental music.

The prelude to Act V is Peer Gynt's homecoming, A
Stormy Night at Sea represents a powerfully drawn sea storm
and shipwreck. A Scene at Night on the Heath expresses
Peer's qualms of conscience. It is a melodrama with chorus
and organ representing balls of yarn, dead leaves, dripping
dew drops, broken stubble, soughing of the air, closing with
the Voice of Ase in the offing, with a few bars from her death
scene. A Hymn sung by the faithful on their way to Whitsun
prayer carries us over to the end with Solveig's Cradle Song.

IV

The chief characteristics of Ibsen's verse are his sparkling
wit, the finish of his style, the flexibility, the richness and the
variety of his rhythm. His rhymes have as much genius in
them as his thoughts. Sometimes his verse is lean and meaty,
like "Macbeth," sometimes it is explosive as "Lear;" at times
it is loquacious as old Chaucer. But always the quality of
Ibsen's verse is fashioned upon the dramatic rather than upon
poetic models. He steers clear of cramping meters and fixed
measures. He uses the short line for vigor and the long line

for grace and strength. Ibsen employs the usual substitution feet, especially the amphibrach, which gives crispness and force, and a natural speech-stress to his verse. Whoever tries to scan his lines by the schoolmarm's finger-tapping rules will come to grief—we take the meaning and the effect of a line or passage as a whole. The scansion test for a line in "Peer Gynt" is always the dramatic one.

The true translator must adopt the very soul of his author. Not only should his version have the ease of the original, but he should transfuse the tone, the spirit, and the fire of his verse, ever compatible with the genius of the English language, embellishing the imagery here, judiciously correcting a defect there.

There are many versions of "Peer Gynt." Some have abused the text in a line-by-line translation, in an effort to reproduce the meter and rhyme, others have degraded into servile "crib" paraphrase. Their rhymes are often made by pronouns or unimportant words, which disappoint the ear and destroy the energy of the line.

This edition of "Peer Gynt" is readable and actable, without any distortion from the normal order of speech, the verse is irregular, the rhymes unobtrusive and irregularly spaced and one line glides gently into another, maintaining at all times, Ibsen's smug conversational style which is the quintessence of this long epic fantasy.

And now, instead of following Ibsen at a distance, I will walk by your side, or just a little ahead of you, and be your guide.

H. M. FINNEY, M.D.

THE CHARACTERS

ASE, a farmer's widow.

PEER GYNT, her son.

TWO OLD WOMEN. ASLAK, the smith. WEDDING GUESTS. A
Cook and Servants. A Fiddler.

THE FARMER AT HEGSTAD and INGRID, his daughter.

A MAN AND WIFE and their daughters—SOLVEIG and HELGA.

A BRIDEGROOM and his parents.

THREE SAETER GIRLS. The Woman in Green.

THE TROLL KING (The Old Man of Dovrë), Lord High Chamberlain, The Rear Admiral, Courtiers, Witches, Maidens, Imps.

A VOICE IN THE DARKNESS. BIRD CRIES. AN UGLY BRAT.

KARI, a housewoman.

MR. COTTON, MONS. BALLON, HERREN von EBERKOPF and
TRUMPETERSTRALE, Travelers.

A THIEF and his Fence (Receiver).

ANITRA, daughter of an Arabian Chief, Arabs, Slaves, Dancing Girls.

SINGING STATUE OF MEMNON. The Sphinx at Gizeh.

PROF. BEGRIFFENFELDT, Ph.D., Director of Madhouse, Cairo.

HUHU, Language Reformer from Malabar Coast.

HUSSEIN, an Oriental Emissary.

A FELLAH with a Royal Mummy.

SEVERAL MADMEN and their Keepers.

A NORWEGIAN SKIPPER and his Crew. A Strange Passenger.

A FUNERAL PARTY, A Pastor, a Bailiff, Mourners.

A BUTTON-MOULDER.

THE THIN MAN.

The action takes place partly in Gudbrandsdal and the neighboring
mountains, partly on the coast of Morocco, in the Sahara Desert, in a
Cairo madhouse, at sea.

ACT I
SCENE I

*A wooded hillside near Ase's farm. A purling millstream
flows down the slope. On the opposite bank stands an old
mill. Peer Gynt, a sturdy lad of twenty comes down the path,
followed by his mother, who is small and slight. She is scolding him roundly.*

ASE

Nonsense, I don't believe a word you say!

PEER
(without stopping)

Come along! The sun waxes warm to-day!

ASE

Not till you swear that it is true!

PEER

Stop driveling. Why swear and argue?

ASE

Because your yarn's a pack of lies!

PEER
(stopping)

Not at all! You should see my prize!

ASE
(confronting him)

Idle braggart, you shame-faced loafer,
When I need you most you disappear;
I gather the crops and feed the flocks,
While you prowl the uplands for game,
Groveling over ice, snow and rocks,
Only to return, battered and lame,

1

Empty-handed, sans coat, sans gear,
And now, poor lad, with meek, downcast eyes
Beguile me with the unseemliest lies.
Come, where did you find the stag, Peer?

PEER

Westward where Gendin rears his hoary mane;
Tall, pristine pines, embalm the morning breeze,
When the breath of the North is on the glen,
Besides a thicket, beneath the trees,
Stood a stately stag, crunching moss—

ASE

(with a scornful laugh)
Indeed!

PEER

Mark me well—now let me proceed.
Over one of the mountain's many streams
Came the flash of an antler's beams.
Stone-still I stood, tongue-tied, amazed;
Close in a mossy copse he grazed—
His nostrils drew in air, soft was his tread.
O, what a steed! So sleek and trim!
A majestic crown, a ten-tined spread!
I'm sure you'll never see the like of him.

ASE

I don't believe a syllable!—

PEER

Bang, and down he fell,
Writhing, kicking, floundering like a steer.
I leaped on his back, seized his left ear,
Thrust my hunting knife in his neck twice.
The mad steed, impatient by the wound,
Bellows, bolts, springs up with a bound,
Tossing me head over heels on the ground,
Pinning me down with his horns like a vise—
His eyes flash fire, clouds from his nostrils glow,
Then, pell-mell along Gendin ridge we go!

ASE
(involuntarily)
Why torture me so!—

PEER
Have you ever seen Gendin ridge?
For miles it skirts the mountain brow,
So sheer and stark, sharp as a sickle's edge;
Above rise glaciers, ice-caps, while below
Cataracts, cascades, tumbling streams and rills
Bicker among the sleeping tarns and hills.
I never rode such a fiery steed;
He outruns blustering Boreas with the speed
Of a demon. Like shadowy shrouds
We imperilously race through the clouds—
The wheeling eagle falls back like a mote
In the sun. Far-off cliffs, beaked peaks glare
And sparkle like gems in the tranced air.
Beneath smoke-grey moraines, ice floes float
And refluent lap the dismal shore—
I heard not a sound, I saw no more,
I only heard as in a dream bound:
The ringing of bells, the dancing of elves,
The music of choirs, heavenly airs,
Above, below, around!

ASE
(dizzy)
God save me!

PEER
As we galloped through ice, snow and mire,
Suddenly from a shelving nook
A screaming, terrified ptarmigan strook
Danzer's cloven hoof—like a vampire
He turns, he cranks with a bound and a leap—
Down, down we plunge into the deep!

(Ase totters and grasps a tree-trunk)

By perilous paths hot grows the pace,
Through deep ravines, shearing the mountain-range,

Through mists and clouds, eerie and strange,
Heaven itself seemed to join the race;
Now, we scatter flocks of sea-gulls astray,
Now downward, ever downward we assay.
But below us figures shimmered,
A brown paunch with white-striped belly!
O mother, 'twas only Danzer and me—
Our own reflection mirrored
In the crystal tarn, rushing up madly,
With the self-same speed to meet us!

ASE
(breathlessly)

Go on, tell me quickly!

PEER

Buck above, buck below clash in the spray,
Sometimes we float, sometimes we swim,
Splashing, floundering, kicking away,
Churning the placid lake high with foam.
I hang on to his stubby tail and pray,
Eagerly we reach the northern-most shore;
He shakes his shanks—the last I see of him;
Wan and weary I wander home.

ASE

Where's the buck? Tell me more!

PEER

Perhaps he's still up there—

(Snaps his fingers, turns on his heels and adds—)

You can have him for all I care!

ASE

You're safe and sound, no cause then for alarm,
I thought, maybe, you broke a leg or arm.
Dear Lord, a mother's thanks, a mother's joy
Be Thine for the safe return of my boy!
Your coat is in shreds, and there's a rent
In your hose. But no matter, I'm content
When I think of what you must have been through—

That wild ride, that hurtling leap! Now you—
(Stops suddenly, looks at him wildeyed and open-mouthed,
*   gropes for words, then blurts out—)*
Out! unvarnished rogue! How you can lie!
But why impose upon your own mother?
You make me so mad, Peer, I could cry!
'Tis one of Gudbrand Glesne's Tales* re-told—
I heard tell when only twenty years old.
My! My! No wonder my boy's so brave and bold!
You found it, no doubt, in some Norge Reader!

PEER

Just a mere coincidence—
I see no resemblance!

ASE

(exasperated)

A lie turned inside out to look like new,
Bustling with adventure, hurly-burly;
You held me spell-bound for a while though
With clever forged conceits and trappings—
Out-flying eagles, hair-splitting frenzy,
And then, climaxing your nefarious yarn
With a dare-devil leap into the tarn—
'Tis an old dish with new trimmings!

PEER

If any man ever said that to me,
I would thrash him roundly.

ASE

(Weeping)

O would to God I lay sleeping
In some cold, cold grave!
Prayers nor tears cannot lave
Your lost soul—beyond redeeming!

PEER

There, there, mother mine!
Right you are about my shortcomings—
All big, black clouds have silver linings!

---

* The Tale is found in Asbjörnsen's "Huldre Eventyr."

ASE

Once I was happy, but now I'm forlorn,
Left a poor widow to fret and to mourn;
My meed is nothing but shame and scorn,
A churlish son burdens like weight of chain—
'Tis unbearable, but why should I complain?

(Weeping again)

What happened to John Gynt's fortune
Which he inherited from your grand-dad?
Remember the big bags of gold strewn
Helter-skelter like grains of sand,
Buying generously large tracts of land,
Riding high in gilded coach and four-in-hand—
Both groom and coachman all velvet-clad?
Remember the sumptuous winter banquet
Where the guests plastered the walls with aquavit?

PEER

Where are the snows of yester-year?

ASE

Silence! Have some respect for your mother!
Look at our house!—almost every window
Plugged with rags—you can hear them rattle!
No shelter, no fodder for the cattle;
The hedges are sere, the rail fences decay
While the fields and the meadows lie fallow,
Overgrown with dock and wild mallow!
We'll be dispossessed, I fear, any day!

PEER

Weep no more, mother, rest your weary throat!
Many a dirge has a sweet merry note,
And Lady Luck boasts more lives than a cat,
Bouncing, rebounding like an acrobat!

ASE

Peer, you're a spunky lad, so fresh and gay,
So rash and cool. I remember the day
A sleek, affable Circuit Rider swore
A precocious lad like you, full of lore,

Would win renown surely in the Sorthing.
With that your gulled father, concurring,
Gave the fat Vicar his best horse and sleigh.
Ah me, Peer, those were the happy days;
Our home was famous for its bounty;
Dignitaries, kinsfolk, landed gentry
Came far and wide to flatter and praise.
Came to taste our choicest Madeira wine,
Feasting and swilling day and night, like swine!
A turn of fortune is friendship's test—
Since then we've never seen a single guest!
Gradually our neighbors gave us the sack,
And "Gold-Bag John" took up his peddler's pack!

(Dries her tears on her apron.)

My boy, you're a husky, strapping lad;
I am so weary from toil and tears;
You should staff and comfort my declining years.
It's time you settled down and be glad
To salvage your father's decaying farm.

(Crying again.)

Heaven knows the little help you've been,
Groveling on the hearth at home to warm
Your lazy bones; what's more, you were seen
Frightening boys and girls out of their wits,
Consorting, fighting with hang-dogs, rowdies,
Humiliating me by your antics—

PEER
(turning away)

Leave me alone!

ASE
(following)
You lie with ease!
Were you not the ringleader at the melee
The other night, down at Lundë?
Someone went berserk. In the encounter
You dislocated Smith Aslak's finger!

PEER

Who told you such lies?

ASE
(hotly)

The cotters heard the cries!

PEER
(rubbing his elbow)

That was me yelling!

ASE

Not you?

PEER

Yes, I got a thrashing!

ASE

What!

PEER

He was no fledgling!

ASE

Who?

PEER

Aslak, the village smithy!

ASE

Shame, I could spit in your face!
Thrashed by a drunken beast! O, the disgrace!
Bah! Peer vanquished by the village smithy!
(Weeping again)
I've suffered hell and humility!
'Tis the last straw, such a calamity!
Poor John Gynt would turn over in his grave!
The smith's husky, but you're as strong and brave!

PEER

Whether I win or lose, you wail!
Soft there, I'll tell you a better tale!
(Laughing)

ASE

What, more lying?

PEER

Yes, just one more, mother.
Now, dry those eyes and stop crying.

(Clenching his left fist)

Look! With this same pair of hands,
I doubled up the snow-shoer smith,
Tossed him in the air—so! on his back he lands,
Hammer-like I swung my good right fist with—

ASE

O, you lusty brawler—you're driving me
To my grave by your tomfoolery!

PEER

No, you're worth a better, nobler fate,
Better times are in store for you, mother.
Dear little mother of mine, have patience.
Take my word for it—only wait,
The old town shall pay you reverence.
Some day you'll be proud of me—I'll be great!

ASE
(contemptuously)

You!

PEER

When fortune strikes, who knows!

ASE

Pshaw! What a slap-happy dreamer!
Why, you can't even mend your own clothes!

PEER
(hotly)

I'll be a King, or Kaiser!

ASE

Heaven help me! Wait, more conceits!
Mark me, sonny, you're losing your wits!

PEER

In time you'll see!

                              ASE
Ho! ho! So you want to be a King,
Or "Puissant Peer" of the Strothing!

                              PEER
Just stick with me!

                              ASE
Silence! You're as mad as a March hare!
You might amount to something, Peer,
If it wasn't for your lying and clowning!
Now, put your wits to work.—I understand
Hegstad's girl fancies you; ask for her hand!
Stop your nonsense. Do a little wooing!

                              PEER
Honest?

                              ASE
          That should be easy sailing;
Gaffer Hegstad's in his dotage, failing;
Ingrid leads her father about by the nose!
                    (Begins to cry again)

She's a rich prize, too, graced with rare charms,
And think of the well-stocked barns and farms!
Why not swap those old weeds for wedding clothes!

                              PEER
                           (briskly)
Come, mother, we'll go a-wooing!

                              ASE
Where?

                              PEER
          To Hegstad's!

                              ASE
                    No use going!
Only friends and guests allowed there!

                              PEER
What do you mean?

ASE

You lost your turn—
It's the early bird that catches the worm!

PEER

How come?

ASE

While you were warming your hands,
Chasing the deer, sailing through the air,
Mads Möen won the girl, and her lands!

PEER

What! The town's sober-sad wall-flower?

ASE

Yes, Mads Möen's going to marry her!

PEER

Wait! I'll get the mare from the meadow!
(Turning to go)

ASE

Never mind—the wedding's tomorrow!

PEER

Pooh! This very evening I'll be there!

ASE

Take it easy! Would you crown our sorrow
With a load of scorn and spite?

PEER

Keep cool! Everything will turn out right!
(Shouting and laughing at the same time)
Upseedaisy! No time to get the mare.
(Lifting her up in his arms)

ASE

Peer, put me down!

PEER

No need for alarum,
I'll take you on my back to Hegstad's farm!
(Wading out into the stream)

ASE

Help! God save us! We'll drown!

PEER

Never! You'll live to see your Peer crowned!

ASE

Rubbish! Here's your crown! *(Thumping his head)*
Such ego!

PEER

Steady now—the bottom's smooth and slippery!

ASE

Ass!

PEER

Hold still, ma! Why all the flurry!
Hold tight, here's the shelving! Up we go!

ASE

Watch your footing!

PEER

Higgledy-piggledy, hop!
We'll play Peer and his reindeer—
I'm Danzer, you're Peer!
(Prancing)

ASE

For Heaven's sake, don't let me drop!
(Wading ashore)

PEER

Here we are now—safe and sound!
Come, give your steed a pretty smack
For the ride you had on his back!

ASE

Here's your reward! *(Boxing his ears.)*

PEER

That was a scurvy whack!

ASE

Put me down!

PEER

First to the wedding;
You're so clever—you do the talking—
Tell Hegstad Mads' a sot, a good-for-nothing—

ASE

Put me down!

PEER

After you've cajoled
The old man, tell him I'm a lad of gold!

ASE

Yes, I'll do all that, and more, I'll swear!
I'll tell him the truth, and I'll not spare
A word about your wrong-doings, you scamp!
And the way you treat your own mother!

PEER

O, will you?

ASE

(Kicking with rage)
I'll talk straight from the shoulder!
I'll have him sic the dog on you, like a tramp!

PEER

Then, I'll go alone to the fray!

ASE

Go ahead! I'll follow, I know the way!

PEER

O no! You're not strong enough!

ASE

What! You know when I'm mad, I'm very tough;
I can crush rocks and stones with one huff!
Now, put me down!

PEER

Yes, if you promise—

ASE

Yes, I'll go to Hegstad's, but get this—
They shall know your true worth—

PEER

In that case you will have to stay here!

ASE

There is nothing you can do to prevent—

PEER

This will hold you for awhile—up there!
(Puts her on mill-house roof. Ase screams.)

ASE

Put me down!

PEER

If you'll only consent—

ASE

Put me down, right away! *(Throws sod at him)*

PEER

If I dared, I'd be glad to help you down! *(Coming closer)*
Sit still, don't rip the tile, stop kicking,
You might slip off and break an arm!

ASE

Beast!

PEER

Please, no more sermons to-day!

ASE

I'll have you changed into a changeling,
And blow you up the chimney!

PEER

Better relent!

ASE

Bah!

PEER

Give my adventure your blessing! *(Going)*

ASE

I'd like to give you a good thrashing,
I hope you break a leg on the way!

PEER

I'm doing this for your own good, mother,
This will give you time to think things over!
(In going, he returns, holds up his finger warningly)

ASE

God help me! He's leaving me up here!
Liar! Reindeer rider! Peer! Peer!
No! He's cutting across the meadow!
Help! I'm slipping! Look out below! *(Screams)*
(Two old women with sacks on their backs, come by.)

FIRST OLD WOMAN

Look! Who's screaming?

ASE

It's me, Ase!

SECOND OLD WOMAN

Well, you're surely sitting on high!

ASE

O, I'll go higher and higher by and by!

FIRST OLD WOMAN

God bless you! May St. Peter find you a place!

ASE

Get a ladder! O, that double-crosser!

SECOND OLD WOMAN

Your son?

ASE

'Tis one of his paltry pranks!

FIRST OLD WOMAN

We'll attest!

ASE

I must go to Hegstad's

SECOND OLD WOMAN
Is he going there?

FIRST OLD WOMAN
Then you'll get even with Peer,
The smith's also going to the farm.

ASE
(Wringing her hands)
God help me! I must save him from harm!

FIRST OLD WOMAN
That's to be feared!

SECOND OLD WOMAN
She's sure out of her head!
Ho Eivind! Anders! Ho! Come here! *(Calling up the hill)*

A MAN'S VOICE
What's wrong?

SECOND OLD WOMAN
Peer's put his mother up there—
On the roof of the old mill-shed!

SCENE II

A hillside covered with bushes and heather. A highway, shut off by a fence, runs at the back. Peer Gynt comes down a path, goes quickly up to the fence, stops and stands looking over the scene beyond.

PEER
Yonder lies Hegstad—if I'd only known.
(Half climbs over the fence, then hesitates)
I wonder if she's happy in her choice?
(Shades his eyes and looks down the road)
Now, the gift-bearing guests swarm like midgets.

I should go home—I can't raise my voice!
                    (Draws back his legs)

Yet their sly whispers sting like hornets!
          (Takes a few steps from fence, plucks a few leaves)

Ah! If I had a bumper of brandy,
Or if I could only see her alone,
Or if I were unknown—a good stiff nip
Would be best, then their jests wouldn't hurt me!
*(Startled, looks around, hides in the bushes. Wedding guests
          on their way to the farm, pass by.)*

A MAN
(To a Woman)
His father's a sot, his mother's so weak!

A WOMAN
A wanton boy—the cause not hard to seek!
     (As they pass on, Peer comes forth and looks after them.)

PEER
(Softly)
Were they talking of me? *(With a forced shrug)*
                    Let them gossip,
They can't talk me dead—and one soon forgets!
*(Lies down on the heath on his back, with his hands under
          his head, gazing up at the sky)*

What a zany cloud! Looks like Pegasus
          Without his wings!
Saddled and bridled with such a proud groom
          Upon his back!
Look! Behind comes an old crone on a broom,
          All dressed in black!
Ho! ho! It's mother! How she can cuss!
          And how she sings!
                    (His eyes gradually close)

King Peer rides at the head of his army,
His horse richly caparisoned in silver,

His long coat's lined with silk accordingly,
At his girdle hangs an embossed dagger,
  Saber, scabbard and gear glisten in the sun—
  None sits so proudly as John Gynt's son!

King Peer's gracious bounty knows no bounds;
Like a farmer jauntily sowing his spring seeds,
He tosses, right and left, shillings and crowns;
Rich grows everyone by his knightly deeds,
  Making the parish rich which once was poor,
  Hail King Peer! re-echoes from door to door!

From far and near the people mill about,
Old warriors at attention solemnly stand,
King Peer! King Peer! they lustily shout—
Many stand with their hats in their hand,
  Women kneel and curtsey, amazed and still,
  Some gaze, some weep, their humble eyes to fill!

King Peer sails across the sea to England;
The Crown Prince warmly greets him on the shore,
England's daughters dance and sing on the strand,
Knights, Dukes, Earls, Lords and Peers, and many more
  Welcome King Peer with garlands of bays,
  Even England's King doffs his crown and says—

ASLAK, THE SMITH
(to companions)

Look! Here's Peer Gynt, the drunken sot!

PEER

What? King!

ASLAK
(leaning over the fence and grinning)

Come, get up, you're a sorry lot!

PEER

Zounds! Aslak, the smith! What now, old trumpet?

ASLAK
(to the others)

Just a hang-over from our Lundë-spree!

PEER
(Springing up)

Leave me alone!

ASLAK

Yes, I'm going, see!
But where have you been? No one has seen
You for six weeks. Hunting for the Troll queen?

PEER

I've been doing unusual things, don't forget!

ASLAK
(winking at the others)

Let's hear them, Peer!

PEER

No, it's a secret!

ASLAK
(pausing)

You're going to the wedding?

PEER

No!

ASLAK

They say
Ingrid was fond of you in a way!

PEER

You dirty dog!

ASLAK
(starting back)

Now don't get so mad!
If she's jilted you, others may be had!
Keep your chin up! Come along to the wedding,
Pretty girls, bewitching widows are waiting!

PEER

Go to—!

ASLAK

There you'll find many dainty dishes!

Good evening, I'll give the bride your best wishes!
> *(They leave, laughing and whispering.)*

PEER
(Looks after them for awhile, shakes his fist defiantly and turns half around.)

I know Ingrid is rich and good and fair,
Fate says she's not for me—but why despair?

> *(Looks at his clothes.)*

My clothes are a sight—tattered and dirty;
If only I had something neat and tidy!

> *(Stamps on the ground.)*

If I had a butcher's grip and skill,
I'd rip their breasts. Out damned hate and ill will!

> *(Looking around suddenly)*

What was that! Who's there? Sounded like a snicker!
No, no, nobody! I'll go home to mother!

> *(Starts to go, stops, moves slowly around towards the fence)*

I hear music. How they swarm about like flies—
Six girls to a man. On to the festival!
I bet poor ma's raving mad as usual!

> *(Stares, listens, leans on fence; now steps up a couple of rails; swings a leg over the fence, rubs his hands and laughs.)*

Hi! That's a polka! Now they dance on the green!
Aye! Only Guttorm can make that violin sing
Like a rippling, tumbling mountain stream!
How they skip and hop and dance in a ring!
Hell-a-fire! I can't miss the festivities.

> *(Jumps down from fence, runs down the road.)*

SCENE III

The Hegstad homestead with the farm buildings in the background. Many wedding guests. A lively dance is going on on the green. The fiddler's seated on a table. The cook stands in the doorway. Maids and servants pass to and fro between the buildings. The older guests gossip in groups here and there.

A WOMAN
(To a group sitting on a pile of logs)
The bride, ah, yes, she's crying a bit;
But that, you know, doesn't mean a whit.

THE COOK
(to another group)
Drink up, folks! We've enough for tonight and tomorrow!

A MAN
Thanks, good neighbor—that's a-plenty, I say!

A LAD
(To the fiddler flying past, holding a lass by the hand)
Go to it, old timer! Play, gypsy, play!

THE GIRL
Saw away, make it ripple over the meadow!

OTHER GIRLS
(Watching a lad dancing and kicking)
That's a high one! *

A GIRL
Nimble as a turtle-dove!

A LAD
(dancing)
The walls are high and wide—only the sky above!

---

*Halling Dance. Indoors it was a great feat to kick the rafters. The Woman in Green (Act II, Scene V) says her father, the Troll King, was a champion kicker. In Prof. Lageman's Commentary on Peer Gynt, we read: "The Men of Valdren were famous for their litheness and vigor when dancing the Halling. They danced it on their heels and on their hams; jumped and kicked, whizzed around on the floor, and managed to hit the goal, so that it resounded through the hall."

THE BRIDEGROOM
*(Comes up whining to his father, who is standing and talking
to some others, and tugs his coat-sleeve.)*
Father, Ingrid refuses to see me!

THE FATHER
What's that?

THE BRIDEGROOM
She's locked herself in her room!

HIS FATHER
See your father-in-law—I can't endure—

THE BRIDEGROOM
He's no help!

HIS FATHER
O what a spineless groom!
(Resumes conversation with friends. Bridegroom sulks away.)

A LAD
(Comes from behind the house)
Girls! Here comes the life of the party—
Peer Gynt!

ASLAK, THE SMITH
(who has just come up)
Who invited him?

THE COOK
No one, I'm sure! *(going)*

ASLAK
(to the girls)
If he speaks to you, take no heed of him!

A GIRL
(To the others)
Just ignore Peer—we'll all look dumb and grin!

PEER GYNT
(Struts jauntily before the crowd, clapping his hands.)
Come girls, which one of you is the best dancer?

A GIRL
(as he approaches her)

Not me!

ANOTHER
(as before)

I am not!

A THIRD
Nor I, either!

PEER
(to a fourth)

How about you? You look blithesome!

THE GIRL

Not this time!

PEER
(to a fifth)
You, good-looking?

THE GIRL
(going)
I'm going home!

PEER

Nonsense! This shindig has only begun!

ASLAK
(Pauses, lowers his voice)

Tough luck, Peer! She's dancing with an old man!

PEER
(turning to an elderly man)

What! All spoken for?

THE MAN
(leaving)
Why not try again!

(Peer Gynt has become subdued. He glances furtively at the

*group. They look but do not speak. When he leaves they only
smile and grin behind his back.)*

PEER
(alone)

Their wily whispers, glances and guffaws
Burn and rasp my soul, like dull saws!

*(He slowly moves along the fence. Solveig leading little Helga
by the hand, comes into the farm-yard with her parents.)*

A MAN
(to another near Peer)

These are newcomers?

THE OTHER
They come from the west.

THE FIRST MAN

From Hedal.

THE OTHER
The little tyke's the keenest!

PEER
*(Good-naturedly confronts the newcomers, points to Solveig
and asks the father:)*

May I dance with your daughter?

THE FATHER
(softly)

Aye, just as soon
As I bid the bride and groom good fortune,
And wish our good host thrift and wealth,
And drink to their everlasting health.

(They go in.)

THE COOK
(offering him a drink)

Well, as long as you're here, try my brandy!

PEER
(looking steadfastly after the newcomers)

Thanks, I'd rather dance. I'm not thirsty!

(The Cook leaves. Peer moves towards the house, laughing.)

O so sweet a face, such homely grace,
Looked shyly at her shoes, then at her apron,
Clinging demurely to her mother's dress;
A Bible, bound by a blue ribbon
In her spotless handkerchief pressed—
I cannot refrain to look on her again!

(Goes into the house)

A LAD

(coming out with several others)

Leaving?

PEER

No!

THE LAD

You're heading for trouble then!

(Takes hold of his shoulders, turns him around)

PEER

Let me pass!

THE LAD

Afraid of the smith, Aslak?

PEER

Of no man!

THE LAD

Watch the smith—he'll pay you back!

(They laugh and move off to the dance)

SOLVEIG

(In the doorway)

Are you the lad who wanted to go dancing?

PEER

Why, of course, don't you remember me asking?
Come along!

(Taking her hand)

SOLVEIG

I can't go far, said mother.

PEER

What! Still tied to your mother's apron-string!

SOLVEIG

Don't laugh!

PEER

You're still mother's little daughter—
Are you grown up?

SOLVEIG

I was confirmed last spring!

PEER

Tell me your name—let's get acquainted!

SOLVEIG

My name's Solveig, and what are you called?

PEER

Peer Gynt!

SOLVEIG
(withdrawing her hand)

Good Heavens!

PEER

You make my ears burn!

SOLVEIG
(leaving)

My garter is loose—I must return!

THE BRIDEGROOM
(Pulling at his mother's gown)

Mother, she will not!

HIS MOTHER

What? Tell me more!

THE BRIDEGROOM

She won't, mother!

HIS MOTHER

What?

THE BRIDEGROOM

Unlock the door!

HIS FATHER
(angrily, but softly)
O, go back to your stall, you silly ass!

HIS MOTHER
Don't scold him, you only embarrass—
(they leave)

A LAD
(with a crowd from the dancing green)
Have a nip, Peer!

PEER
No!

THE LAD
Only a drop.

PEER
(looking darkly at him)
Have you some?

THE LAD
(drinking from a flask)
Ah, that's got a wallop!

PEER
Give me a sip! *(drinking)*

ANOTHER LAD
Now you must try mine!

PEER
No!

THE LAD
Come, come, Peer, don't be so asinine!
Have a swig!

PEER
Well, I can hardly decline! *(drinks)*

A GIRL
(half aloud)
Come, let's go!

PEER
Surely you're not afraid?

A THIRD LAD
Who isn't afraid of you?

A FOURTH
At Lundë
You displayed some clever tricks!

PEER
I must have the proper spirit!

FIRST LAD
(whispering)
He's slipping fast!

SEVERAL OTHERS
(forming a circle)
Come now, Peer, recite
One of your best!

PEER
Tomorrow!

THE OTHERS
No, tonight!

A GIRL
Can you conjure the devil?

PEER
That's quite right!

A MAN
As old as the hills, boy—an old chestnut!

PEER
Liar! Don't forget there's only one Peer.
Once I conjured the devil into a nut—
It was worm-bored!

SEVERAL
(laughing)
That's easy to figure out!

PEER

He raved, swore and wept during the bedlam,
He promised me this and that!

ONE IN THE CROWD
'Twas quite a bout!

PEER

Aye, I used my black-magic like a seer,
And plugged up the hole with a pin;
Then he'd put, put, like a water-ram,
Rumbling, grumbling, tumbling—'twas a sin!

A GIRL

Honest?

PEER
He made more noise than a bumble-bee!

THE GIRL
Still got him in the nut?

PEER
No, he took leave.
The devil just vanished into the air;
The feud the smith bears, stems from there!

A LAD

Why?

PEER
Because I took him to the smithy
To have him crack the nut and set him free;
I laid it on the anvil, and as you know,
Aslak is muscle-bound; then with a heave
And a ho, he double-swung his hammer!

A VOICE FROM THE CROWD
Did you free the viper?

PEER
He smote like Samson!
But the devil put up a fight, of course.
In a fiery blast he tore off the roof!

SEVERAL VOICES

And the smith?

PEER

Stood there aghast—his hands scorched,
And from that day we've never been friendly.

(All laugh.)

SOMEONE

Aye, well spun!

OTHERS

Good, if he has any proof!

PEER

My veracity doubted?

A MAN

Why, no!
But it sounds like an old wives' tale!

PEER

Liar! But never mind!

THE MAN

Consider the source!

PEER

(turning his head)

I can ride through the air like a whirlwind,
On fiery steeds—there's nothing I can't do!

ONE OF THE CROWD
(Roars of laughter)

Ride a cloud?

A MAN

Mind if I go on one of your jaunts?

PEER

Laugh! Laugh! Spare your sinister taunts!
Some day I'll ride like a tempest over you all,
And at my feet the whole countryside shall fall.

AN ELDERLY MAN

A little tetched in the head!

ANOTHER
Silly!

A THIRD
Arrogant!

A FOURTH
Liar!

PEER
(threatening them)
Wait! Some day you shall see!

A MAN
(intoxicated)
Ha, wait fool, you'll soon get a good dusting!

OTHERS
A pair of black eyes, too, and a drubbing!
*(They disperse—the older ones angry, and the youngsters
jeering and laughing.)*

THE BRIDEGROOM
(coming close)
Is it true, then, you can ride on a cloud?

PEER
(curtly)
Yes, Mads, but you haven't seen anything yet!

THE BRIDEGROOM
Have you, indeed, such an invisible shroud?

PEER
I use an Invisible Hat, sometimes I ride
My Black Horse!
(Leaves as Solveig and Helga cross the courtyard.)
I see you didn't forget.
(Taking Solveig by the hand)
Now I'll show you how to dance the Halling.

SOLVEIG
No, please!

PEER

Why?

SOLVEIG

You're so blustering!

PEER

The reindeer grows warm when summer is near!
Come along, lass! On to the Halling!

SOLVEIG

I'm afraid!

PEER

Of what?

SOLVEIG

I smell liquor! *(leaving)*

PEER

Why didn't I cut their throats from ear to ear!

THE BRIDEGROOM

Ah, Peer—give me a hand, rescue my bride!

PEER

(absently)

The bride! Where?

THE BRIDEGROOM

Locked up!

PEER

So that's why you're alone!

THE BRIDEGROOM

Come, Peer, please—do me this one favor!

PEER

No! Poor Peer has troubles of his own!
   (A flash comes to him and he says softly but abruptly)
Ingrid locked up!
                    (Going up to Solveig)
                    Have you changed your mind?
              (She starts to go; he confronts her)
You're ashamed because I look like a vagrant!

SOLVEIG

(hastily)

That is not true—you only spoke *your* mind!
As a man thinketh, so is he, they say!

PEER

You belittled and avoided me tonight—
'Tis true, I drank, but only for spite.
Your attitude hurt me deeply. Come this way!

SOLVEIG

I cannot go!

PEER

Afraid?

SOLVEIG

Father's adamant!

PEER

I surmised that; he's so sanctimonious!
He never swears—just "avers"—and so pious!

SOLVEIG

What shall I say?

PEER

Why do you hang your head
And blush so? Ah, I understand!

SOLVEIG

Let me go!

PEER

(In a low, menacing tone)

Sometime along about the midnight hour,
When the old church clock echoes from the tower,
When the horned moon shines down in tranced air,
When all is still and the sky is bare,
When all the household has gone to sleep,
I'll steal through the window or up the stair;
But if you hear a fearful growl or moan,
It's not the prowling cat, but I alone;
I'll stifle your breath, and drain your veins dry,

I'll steal your little sister if she makes a peep,
I'll pinch you blue, I'll scratch you till you cry;
Beware! I'm a Werewolf when the horn's on the moon!
   (Changes his tone entreatingly as if in fear)
Come, dance with me!

SOLVEIG
(looking at him darkly)
It's terrible the way you acted!
(leaving)

THE BRIDEGROOM
(sidling up again)

I'll give you an ox instead!

PEER
Come, let's go!

*(They go behind the house. At the same time a crowd from
the dance, most of them drunk, come forward, shouting and
unruly. Solveig, Helga and their parents and some elderly
people come out on the porch.)*

THE COOK
(to the smith, the leader)

Keep the peace!

THE SMITH
(pulling off his coat)
No! I've heard enough; we'll fight it out!

SOME VOICES

Let them fight!

OTHERS
Make it a wrestling bout!

THE SMITH

Fists, only fists shall decide this case!

SOLVEIG'S FATHER

Control yourself, man!

HELGA
Will they beat him, mother?

A LAD

No, just taunt him!

ANOTHER

Chase him home!

A LAD

Spit in his face!

FOURTH LAD
(to the smith)

Getting cold feet, smith?

THE SMITH
(Throwing down coat)

I'll slaughter the scoundrel!

SOLVEIG'S MOTHER
(to Solveig)

See how they treat the windbag, daughter?

ASE
(Coming up with a staff in her hand)

Is that good-for-nothing son of mine here?
I'm going to give him a sound thrashing!

THE SMITH
(rolling up his sleeves)

Pshaw Ase, you'll need a larger cudgel!

SOME OF THE CROWD

The smith will thrash him!

OTHERS

Soundly!

THE SMITH
(spitting on his hands)

It's death!

ASE

Just try it! Ase and I have claws and teeth!
Where is he? *(calling)* Peer! Peer!

THE BRIDEGROOM
(Running up excitedly)
For God's sake, come quick!

HIS FATHER
Now, what's the trouble?

THE BRIDEGROOM
Oh! Peer Gynt's—

ASE
(screaming)
Have you slain my Peer?

THE BRIDEGROOM
No! But look! look on the hillside!

THE CROWD
With the bride!

ASE
(dropping her staff)
Beast!

THE SMITH
(thunderstruck)
Sure-footed as a goat!

THE BRIDEGROOM
My God! Look, he shoulders her like a shoat!

ASE
(shaking her fist at him)
I hope you fall and break your head!
(Screaming) Watch your footing!

INGRID'S FATHER
(Comes on bareheaded, white with rage.)
I'll have his life for this kidnapping!

ASE
O no! If I let you—God strike me dead!

ACT II

SCENE I

*Early morning, high up in the mountains. Peer comes hastily
and sullenly down a narrow path. Ingrid, still wearing some
of her bridal finery, tries to hold him back.*

PEER GYNT

Go home!

INGRID
(weeping)
Now, I find your love was feigned!

PEER

Go away!

INGRID
(wringing her hands)
Love quickly lost, quickly gained!

PEER

The devil take all remembrances!
The devil take all vixen-glances!
All, save one!

INGRID

And who is she?

PEER

A lovely maid!

INGRID

Who is it, pray?

PEER

Never mind, return to Hegstad!

INGRID

Impossible!

PEER

I'd lief be a castaway!

INGRID

Wooed, deflowered, forsaken in a night!

PEER

Well, what have you to offer?

INGRID

Farms, lands and more I proffer!

PEER

Do you have dreamy blue eyes?
Do you carry a bible in your kercher?
Does your golden hair hang in curls?
Do you hold on to your mother?
Do you watch little sister like other girls,
And a thousand other courtesies?
Speak!

INGRID

No, but—

PEER

Were you ever confirmed?

INGRID

No, Peer!

PEER

Are you bashful and shy?
If I beg, do you deny?

INGRID

You're out of your mind!

PEER

Does your presence sanctify?

INGRID

No, but—

PEER

Then, you really have nothing to offer! *(going)*

INGRID
(Blocking his way)
You know, of course, the penalty—take wealth
And honor and me, or else—

PEER
I spurn your gold!

INGRID
(bursting into tears)
Wash your foul deed away!

PEER
Bad as I, tenfold!

INGRID
I was desperate, Peer!

PEER
O, foul appetite!

INGRID
You know the price—death!

PEER
O, tell-tale night!

INGRID
Your mind's made up?

PEER
Aye, until doomsday!

INGRID
(descending)
We'll see! The Hegstads will make you pay!

PEER
The devil take all remembrances!
The devil take all vixen-glances! All save one!

INGRID
(calls up mockingly)
All save one!

PEER
Yes, all save one!
(They separate)

SCENE II

On a boggy moorland, close by a mountain tarn. A storm is
brewing. In despair, Ase is calling and looking over the
moor. Solveig can hardly keep up with her. Solveig's parents
and Helga struggle behind.

ASE
(Waving her arms and tearing her hair.)

Ah me! Misfortune is swift of foot!
Aye, even the elements dog my steps!
The lowering fog scowls like a brute
Over moor and mountain-top, and creeps
  Damply across the tarn! O my son, my son!
  I can't live without him! I'm undone!

Now, the rabble cry out for punishment!
God forbid! Why do widows suffer most?
And He alone knows my boy's penitent!
He's my all-in-all, without him I'm lost!
  O the dolt! To let the devil lead him on!
  It's incredible to yield to temptation!

    (Turns to Solveig)

For you must know his father was a sot.
John Gynt became a byword—soon died.
And his fortune slowly dwindled to naught,
And left us alone—unpitied, unrespected!
  My life has been one of wormwood and gall,
  And I sigh afresh for days beyond recall!

But Peer and I were copartners in our need;
We stayed at home and took our exile with a sigh.
I was too frail to stand the strain; indeed,
Sometimes confused, I would both laugh and cry
  When I met fate face to face, and to reconcile
  The thought you've lost everything worth while!

Some take to brandy, others have their vices;
We took comfort in the sagas of the vikings,
Of princesses, knights and goblins, trolls and fairies,
And many more that solitude always brings.
      Aye, of stolen brides, too, but whoever suspected
      That those old wives' tales would stick in his head!

(In terror)

Ha! What a scream! Sounds more like a troll!
Peer! Peer! Look there on the top of the knoll!

(She runs to the top of a little hill and looks over the tarn)
Not a sign!

THE FATHER
(quietly)
Too bad—I thought 'twas your boy!

ASE
(weeping)
Peer! O my lost lamb, my boy!

THE FATHER
(softly)

Verily, lost!

ASE
Don't talk so reverential!
He's so clever—he has no equal!

THE FATHER
Foolish woman!

ASE
Yes, yes, you're quite right,
But he's no fool—just a big wayward boy!

THE FATHER
(softly)
He's been weighed in the balance and found wanting!

ASE
(in anguish)
No! Christ made the widow's heart to sing for joy!

THE FATHER
Do you think he feels the weight of his sinning?

ASE
(eagerly)
No, but he can ride through the air at night!

THE MOTHER
What was that?

THE FATHER
O what are you saying?

ASE
There's nothing my Peer cannot do easily—
That is, if he lives long enough—you shall see!

THE FATHER
But the Lord says, The wages of sin is death!

ASE
(shrieking)
O God's not as bad as that—save your breath!

THE FATHER
Sometimes, widow, they repent in the gaol!

ASE
(confused)
At times you speak so strange—I feel dizzy!
We must find **him!**

THE FATHER
To save his soul!

ASE
And body!
We must search the tarn, the moor, the lowland!
If the trolls have him, we must toll the bell!

THE FATHER
Ha!—here's a cowpath!

ASE

Christ reward you well!

THE FATHER

It's my Christian duty to give you a hand!

ASE

Fie on the others—they're only heathen!
Only you and your family act like brethren!

THE FATHER

They knew him too well—'twas noised about
He was a wanton lad.

ASE

Jealous, no doubt!
And to think his very life is now at stake!

THE FATHER

Soft! Here's a footprint!

ASE

It leads to the lake!

THE FATHER

We'd better separate.
(He and his wife go on ahead)

SOLVEIG

(to Ase)
Come, tell me more!

ASE

(drying her eyes)
Of Peer, you mean?

SOLVEIG

Yes, tell me all, I implore!

ASE

(smiles, tosses her head)
'Twould tire you lass—it's a long, long story.

SOLVEIG

No, Mother Ase, go on, tell it slowly!

SCENE III

Late in the day, upon a bare hillock. Long shadows fall over the landscape. Snowcapped mountains in the background.

PEER GYNT
(Comes running at full speed, stops short on the knoll.)

They're after me now—I can hear their yells!
The rabble will soon be on my back!
They're armed with guns, stones and cudgels,
And gaffer Hegstad's leading the pack!
>   But ah, you're not fighting the smith now, Peer!
>   This is life! I feel as strong as a bear!

(Thumps his chest and leaps in the air.)

To strike, to shatter! Breast a waterfall!
To beat, to break! Uproot the fir-tree!
To tear and twist its roots into a ball!
This is life! It hardens like adversity!
>   It's like a game—you win or lose or pass!
>   To hell with lying! The devil's an ass!

THREE SAETER GIRLS
(Come over the hill, shouting and singing.)

Holla! Trond and Bard and Kare,
Come, dance! Drive away dull care!

PEER

To whom are you calling?

THE GIRLS
The trolls, of course!

FIRST GIRL

Trond, come down!

SECOND GIRL
Bard, come with force!

THIRD GIRL

Now our cots are empty which once were full!

FIRST GIRL

Might makes right!

SECOND GIRL

No, right makes might!

THIRD GIRL

If no lads, we bed with the trolls at night!

PEER

Where are the lads?

ALL THREE GIRLS
(with a horse-laugh)
O it's so pitiful!

FIRST GIRL

Mine called me darling, and sweetheart, too,
And then eloped with a grey-haired widow!

SECOND GIRL

Mine met a gypsy lass twice his age,
Now they trek from village to village!

THIRD GIRL

Mine strangled our brat born out of wedlock,
And they chopped off his head on the block!

THE GIRLS

Holla! Trond and Bard and Kare!
Come, troll pack, come to our saeter!

PEER
(Suddenly leaps in the midst of them)
Girls, I am a troll, and have three heads!

THE GIRLS

How nice!

PEER

I'll warm your feet and man your beds!

FIRST GIRL

To the hut!

SECOND GIRL

We have mead!

PEER

We'll drain it down!

THIRD GIRL

Every cot shall be busy tonight!

SECOND GIRL
(kissing him)

Ah, he sparkles like a meteor-light!

THIRD GIRL
(as before)

Like a diamond in the King's crown!

PEER
(Dancing in the midst of them)

They say one flower never makes a garland,
But *three* is a bouquet in any hand!

THE GIRLS

Holla! Trond, and Bard and Kare,
Come, sleep tonight with your lover!

*(They thumb their noses mockingly at the mountain tops and
leave, singing and dancing.)*

SCENE IV

*Sunset among the Rondë Mountains. Glittering snow peaks
all around.*

PEER GYNT
(Dizzy, confused)

Tower over tower is rising
    With a glittering gate;
Now glow together on the ceiling,
    Now slowly separate.

The noisy cock on the wind-vane lifts
        Its burnished wings for flight,
Sailing among the shadowy cliffs,
        Locked in the mountain height.

What are those towering trunks and tree-roots
        Tossed on the sunset glow?
No! It's a heron-footed warrior that struts
        Over the mountain brow.

I see a nebulous light like a rainbow,
        And I hear bells ringing;
I seem to feel a sudden weight of woe,
        My head's hot and throbbing!

                (Sinks down)

A break-neck flight over Gendin ridge,
        Romancing and lies;
Fled with a bride up the steepest ledge,
        Hunted by hounds and spies;
Aye, drunk for a day and a night,
        Wooing trolls and their like!

                (Gazes long upwards)

There go wild geese, migrating to the South,
        Now wheels the brown eagle;
While I count the time and suck a tooth,
        To fathom the riddle!

                (Springs up)

I'll fly away with them. Come, Boreas!
        Cleanse me in your keenest wind!
I'll lave my sins on the nearest mountain-pass,
        And ride, ride clear of mind!

I'll soar over the fields, far over the sea—
        Aye, as far as England!
But don't wait for me, girls. I must see
        The girls on England's strand!
Now, where did the big brown eagle go?
Vanished! Only the devil would know!

Ho, there's the top of a gilded tower!
      It rises out of the ruins.
A gateway stands in a lofty bower,
      Ah, it's real, genuine!

It's Rasmus Gynt's Palace—the pride of his eye!
      No clots in the windows;
The old fence is gone—bright casements light the sky,
      Ha! Old cronies rub elbows.

(He sighs)

Now, the Vicar's tapping his knife on the glass,
      The Captain smashes his bottle,
And breaks the mirror in bits! Let it pass,
      Mother, let them guzzle!

'Tis the rich John Gynt giving a banquet!
      All hail the House of Gynt!
Why do they shout and call? Now it's quiet—
      The Vicar calls for Peer Gynt!

They lift their glasses—the Vicar gives a toast—
      Here's to the scion of old Gynt!
Great shall be thy name, boy, from coast to coast,
      And richer, too, than a mint.

(Leaps forward, runs against a rock and falls down.)

SCENE V

A wooded hillside with great soughing trees. Stars gleam through the foliage. Birds sing in the treetops. A Woman in Green crosses the slopes, followed by Peer Gynt making all kinds of cajoling antics.

THE WOMAN IN GREEN
(Stops and turns around.)

Is it true?

PEER GYNT
(Drawing his finger across his throat)
I mean every word, I swear.
As true as you're a sweet lass, my little lamb.
Will you have me? You'll see how nice I am;
You'll never have to spin or weave, instead
You'll be well provided for, and well fed,
And I promise never to pull your hair—

THE WOMAN IN GREEN
Nor beat me?

PEER
O, I never heard of such a thing!
Who ever heard of a king's son striking a lady?

THE WOMAN IN GREEN
A king's son?

PEER
Yes!

THE WOMAN IN GREEN
My father's the Dovrë King!

PEER
Well, well! How fortunate! How timely!

THE WOMAN IN GREEN
My father has his castle in the mountains!

PEER
My mother's palace has forty fountains!

THE WOMAN IN GREEN
Do you know my father? He's King Brosë.

PEER
Do you know my mother? She's Queen Ase!

THE WOMAN IN GREEN
The mountains crack when my father's angry!

PEER
The heavens weep when my mother's unruly!

THE WOMAN IN GREEN
My father's the champion Halling kicker!

PEER
My mother can ford the swiftest river!

THE WOMAN IN GREEN
Have you any other clothes than those weeds?

PEER
Pshaw! You should see my imported English tweeds!

THE WOMAN IN GREEN
My every day dresses are of silk and gold.

PEER
Posh! More like grass trimmed with marigold.

THE WOMAN IN GREEN
Now, before you enter our domain,
It's an old custom that all our worldly goods
Have a two-fold shape—everything looks inane,
Everything's upside down, topsy-turvy—
In our little kingdom over the lea.
So when you see our palace, parks and woods,
Don't think for a moment it's a murky moraine.

PEER
Tut, tut woman! A mere coincidence.
Every sprawling log's a sturdy oak fence,
Every plowed furrow is only wild mallow,
Every window but clots and rags in Ase's manse.

THE WOMAN IN GREEN
Ugly seems fair, while black seems white.

PEER
Big seems small, often dull seems bright.

THE WOMAN IN GREEN
(Falling on his neck.)
O Peer! We're amazingly mated!

PEER
As the hand fits the glove, the hair the comb!

THE WOMAN IN GREEN
(Calling over the hillside)

Bridal steed! Bridal steed! Come, come home!

*(An oversized pig comes on with a rope's end for a bridle
and an old sock for a saddle. Peer vaults in the saddle and
puts The Woman In Green in front of him.)*

PEER

Hoopla! We're magnificently stied!
Giddyap! Giddyap! To the King with all speed!

THE WOMAN IN GREEN
(mushily)

I was only a poor King's daughter, and so Green!
But now, noble Prince, I feel like a Queen!

PEER
(Whipping up the pig)

A good rider is known by his steed!

SCENE VI

*The Royal Hall of the King of the Dovrë Trolls. A great
gathering of Trolls—dignitaries, witches, maidens, and imps.
The King, crowned, scepter in hand, sits on his throne with
his children and kinsfolk on either side. Great confusion.*

TROLL COURTIERS

Kill him! Kill the Christian philanderer!
He's beguiled the King's favorite daughter!

TROLL IMP

Chop off his hand!

ANOTHER

Let me at the nit-wit!

TROLL MAIDEN

I'll pinch him black and blue till he groans!

TROLL WITCH
(with a ladle)
So lean—he's only good for soup and bones!

ANOTHER WITCH
(With a cleaver)
Give him forty lashes, or roast him on the spit!

TROLL KING
Quiet, good folks! *(Bids his counsellors to come closer.)*
                  Let's cool off awhile.
We're not as prosperous as we used to be;
We never know what's above or beneath—
Nothing's everlasting, and don't forget
This young cock-a-hoop may become an asset;
It's true he has but only one head,
And my daughter's in the same predicament.
Three-headed Trolls, it seems, are out of style,
Even two-headers are scarce as hen's teeth,
And they, too, are very indifferent.
                  (To Peer)
So you want my daughter? Is that your plea?

PEER GYNT
Yes, and your realm for dowry, I plead.

TROLL KING
You shall have half of my estate anon,
And the other half when I'm dead and gone.

PEER
I'm satisfied with that.

TROLL KING
                  Not so fast, my son,
Now, you've got a few pledges to give,
Break one of them, our Troll-pact's broken,
And the Rondë-folks will skin you alive.
First of all, think naught of the outside world—
From now on it's out of bounds, forbidden—
Shun the day, its sunlight and life's giddy whirl.

PEER

Only call me King, as my dignity permits.

TROLL KING
(arising)
Next the Lord High Chamberlain will test your wits.

LORD HIGH CHAMBERLAIN
Let's see if you've got a wisdom tooth
That can crack the King's riddle-nut.

TROLL KING
How do you differ from us Trolls? Tell the truth.

PEER

It seems to me they don't vary a toot;
The big ones whack you, the little ones slap—
We differ only in how we play the game.

TROLL KING
Very good—in that we certainly agree.
Yet night is night and day is day, you see,
But there's a slight difference, just the same
And this is it—you Christians always exclaim,
"Man, be thyself!"—downright skimble-skramble stuff;
But our Troll-saw goes, "Trolls, be thyself—enough!"

LORD HIGH CHAMBERLAIN
Can you figure it out?

PEER
It has me on the floor!

TROLL KING
"Enough's" a most cogent word in our land,
Wear it ever on your head like a brand.

PEER
(scratching his head)
Well, but—

TROLL KING
It must, if you would be my successor.

PEER
So mote it be—if it comes with a wife.

TROLL KING
Furthermore, Prince Peer, you must now learn
To appreciate our homely simple life.
(He nods and two trolls with pigs' heads and white night-
hoods serve food and drink.)
The cow gives cakes, and the ox gives mead,
Whether they taste sweet or sour, take no heed—
It's all home-brewed, too—we all take our turn.

PEER
(pushing the stuff away)
The devil take your home-brewed stuff,
And your uncouth ways—enough is enough!

TROLL KING
See this beautiful gold bowl—it likewise
Goes with the bride—a consolation prize.

PEER
(meditatively)
Of course, one should always curb his humor,
And, perhaps, the mead will taste better.
(Drinks)

TROLL KING
That was sensibly said. But why do you spit?

PEER
O that's just a force of habit!

TROLL KING
And next, you must discard those rags;
Furthermore, in *this* every Trollman brags,
Everything's Troll-made, not a stitch from the dale
Except the silk bow for the end of your tail.

PEER
(repulsively)
I never had a tail!

TROLL KING
(arising)
You shall have one!
Rear Admiral! Affix my Royal Tail
In the customary manner!

PEER
(indignantly)
I'll have none!

TROLL KING
No one courts my daughter without his Troll-tail!

PEER
(rantingly)
What! Turn me into a beast!

TROLL KING
O no, my son,
This makes you an acceptable wooer;
It's the badge, too, of very high honor,
And the bow's of beautiful orange color!

PEER
(meditatively)
Man, after all, is an imitative creature;
'Tis but a question of give and take, that's sure,
So, tie away!

TROLL KING
Now, you're quite sensible.

LORD HIGH CHAMBERLAIN
Just wig-wag slowly—that's true Troll style!

PEER
(peevishly)
Ha! do you wish me to practice for awhile?
Must I also give up my Christian faith?

TROLL KING
No! "Have faith in thyself—enough!" the Troll saith.
Your faith is free, and you pay no toll.

By his cut and dress you know the Troll—
We're all for one, and one for all;
What you call faith, forsooth, we call thrall!

PEER

In spite of your terms, you're quite fair-minded,
Much more reasonable than I expected.

TROLL KING

We Troll-folks are better than our reputation.
Here, again, we differ from the common herd.
Now, we'll entertain our son with inspired
Music and dance. To the throne! Summon
Dancing maid, and music maid and harp!
On with the dance! Make it loud and sharp!

(Music and a dance)

LORD HIGH CHAMBERLAIN

Do you like it?

PEER

Like it? H'm!—

TROLL KING

Speak without fear!

PEER

Preposterous! Monstrous! And such gear!
An old bell-cow plucking the harp!
A sow in socks trying to dance and carp!

COURTIERS

Eat him!

TROLL KING

He only sees through Christian eyes!

TROLL MAIDENS

Pluck them out! Cut off his long ears!

WOMAN IN GREEN
(weeping)

O! O! Must we put up with his jeers,
While we so gaily dance and sing?

PEER

O ho! It's you my bride, what a surprise!
'Twas only one of our Christian tavern jokes!

WOMAN IN GREEN

Only a jest?

PEER

Yes, you acted like city folks!

TROLL KING

Ah, nature's a very persistent thing.
It sticks to us as long as we live;
Wounded, we get a gash that soon heals,
Save naught but a lone scar remaining.
My son, now, is a most willing soul;
He's discarded his Christian clothes,
Drank mead from Dovrë's golden bowl,
Wears graciously his gay Troll-tail,
So accommodating in everything,
Who'd thought Old Adam in him could survive.
But lo! in two shakes of a dead lamb's tail,
He's back again! This calls for radical treatment—
We must find a cure for his ailment!

PEER

What now, old goat?

TROLL KING

I'll just nick your left eye, like a stye.
You'll be cock-eyed, then, in one eye—
When you look down, you're looking at the sky,
And vice-versa, as you Christians say;
Then your right window-pane I'll break!

PEER

More horse-play!

TROLL KING

(Laying some instruments on the table)
See this glazier's tool?
I'll also fit you with a pair of horse-blinkers—
That'll keep you from flirting sideways,
Or seeing our buxom strumming Trollers!

PEER

Hog-wash!

LORD HIGH CHAMBERLAIN

Silence! Hear the Dovrë King speak!
'Tis he who's the wiseman, and you the fool!

TROLL KING

Ah! Just think of the grief and the tears,
Prince Peer, you'll save in the coming years,
And remember, too, the eyes are the source
Of man's constant flood of sweet and sour tears!

PEER

That's true! The Good Book has it right;
Quotha—if thine eye offend thee, pluck it out!
How soon, King, will I regain my sight?

TROLL KING

That's gone forever!

PEER

Enough! this is worse!

TROLL KING

Going?

PEER

Yes, I can't stand it any longer!

TROLL KING

Not so fast! Your exit's fraught with danger,
Troll-gates swing inwards only, never out!

PEER

You'll surely not detain me by force?

TROLL KING

Come, my son, listen to the voice of reason.
You have a wholesome flair for Trolldom,
You now act, look and talk like a troll;
Once a Troll always a Troll, my son!

PEER

Yes, I can tolerate the mountain-troll
For a bride, a flourishing kingdom, all mine;

I can sacrifice a little pride with ease,
But there's a limit to all things, that's sure;
I accepted the tail with some disdain,
But that I can adjust as I please;
My breeches I've dropped, they're old, tattered,
I can don them again and be myself;
And I can quickly slip my Troll-tow;
I can still swear a cow's a maid now;
Aye, an oath's not difficult to endure,
But to know you're tied up here for life,
And can't even die like a Christian,
Never beat a retreat or take French leave,
King Troll, this is where Peer draws a line!

TROLL KING

Now, you young whipper-snapper, I'm getting mad,
I'm in no mood for any tomfoolery!
Do you know who I am? How could you deceive
My poor daughter? You're a scurvy lad!

PEER

You lie!

TROLL KING
You must marry her!

PEER
Do you accuse me?

TROLL KING

Your heart's full of lust!

PEER
(with a snort)
That doesn't mean a whit!

TROLL KING

Your human-kind hasn't changed a bit,
You prate of your spirit—nothing matters,
Except what your hands cannot seize!
So you think lust doesn't matter! You'll see!
Just wait! You shall see with your own eyes!

PEER

Your hook's baited with too many lies!

TROLL KING

Inside of a year you'll be a father!

PEER

Open the gates before I settle matters!

TROLL KING

We'll send the brat after you in a goat's skin!

PEER

(mopping his brow)

Wake up, Peer!

TROLL KING

Shall we send him to your palace?

PEER

Send him anywhere!

TROLL KING

Well, well, what a slacker!
What's done is done, but these mongrels grow
Up quickly. Some day he'll look for his kin!

PEER

Come, old man, don't act like a jackass!
Let's compromise; listen to reason, lass!
I'm not rich nor a prince with a palace!
Do what you will, you'll lose in the end, I vow.

TROLL KING

(Looks at Peer contemptuously for awhile and exclaims)
Trollers, dash him to pieces on the rocks, now!

TROLL IMPS

O dad, first let's play hoot-owls and bats,
Or the green-eyed mouse and kit-cats.

TROLL KING

Quickly. Good-night! I'm mad and sleepy!

PEER
(chased by Imps)
You little brats! *(Tries to climb up chimney.)*

IMPS
Punish him, nixies, sorely!

PEER
(tries to slip down cellar)
Worse than forty cats!

IMPS
Plug the holes, quickly!

TROLL COURTIER
Ha, ha! Kids will be kids.

PEER
(Struggling with Imp trying to bite his ear)
Le'me go, you tadpole!

TROLL COURTIER
(rapping Peer across the hand)
Tut, tut! That's the King's son!

PEER
Ah, a rat-hole! *(Runs for it)*

IMPS
Head him off, pixies! We've got him on the skids!

PEER
These Imps are far worse than the Old One!

IMPS
Clip him, nixies!

PEER
(rushing around)
O were I only a mouse!

IMPS
(closing in)
Close in, sharply!

PEER

I wish I were a louse! *(falls)*

IMPS

Pluck out his eyes!

PEER

(buried in the heap)
Help, mother, ring the bells,
Save your Peer ere he dies!

IMPS

Hark! The bells, the bells, the Black-frock's cow-bells!

*(Yelling and shrieking the Trolls flee.
The palace collapses—everything disappears.)*

SCENE VII

*Pitch darkness. Peer Gynt is heard beating about him with a
large bough.*

PEER GYNT

Stand! Who are you?

A VOICE IN THE DARKNESS
Myself!

PEER

Out of my way!

THE VOICE

Go around—this place isn't large enough for us two!

PEER

(Trying another way; gets a bump)
Who are you? Friend or foe?

THE VOICE
Myself! Are *you* Peer?

PEER

I say what I like!
Look to yourself! When I strike, I strike!
King Saul slew hundreds, King Peer thousands more!
Again, who are you?

(Slashing about wildly)

THE VOICE
Myself!

PEER

You talk nonsense!
I can't make head or tail out of what you say!
Who are you? Speak!

THE VOICE
The Great Boyg I'm known.

PEER

Pshaw! No fooling, the Great Boyg looks grey,
What looked black before. Clear out, boor!

THE VOICE
Go round about, and save yourself trouble, Peer.

PEER
(slashing)

No! Right through!
He's down at last! *(Bumps into something)*
Here's my chance!

THE VOICE
I'm the Boyg, Peer Gynt, the one and only one!
The unwounded, unhurt, dead Boyg, but much alive!

PEER
(throws away bough)

My sword's charmed! I'll use my fists! Come, I'll rive—
(struggling)

THE VOICE
Better stick to your fists, trust to brawn!
Ho, ho! You may live to see the dawn!

PEER
(falls back)

Backwards or forwards—it's just as far!
In and out, round and round, side to side!
He's here, he's there, he's everywhere!
I'm down, I slide; I'm up, I turn, I glide!
Come out Boyg, fight like a man, wherever you are!

THE VOICE

In time.

PEER
(groping)

Neither dead or alive, yet so eerie;
No form, no shape, no nothing—just a whisper;
I'd as lief wrestle with a surprised bear.
Come, strike back!
(Screams)

THE VOICE
The Boyg's not mad, Peer.

PEER

Strike, I say!

THE VOICE
The Boyg never strikes!

PEER
I'll get you yet!

THE VOICE
I always win without force, don't forget!

PEER

I'd rather fight with a troll, imp or nixie!
Give me something, somebody I can see!
It's snoring now! Boyg!

THE VOICE
What?

PEER
Come fight, you varlet!

THE VOICE

The Great Boyg conquers eventually.

PEER

(clawing, biting own arms)

Nails and teeth in my flesh. Ha! That's good!
I must feel the drip, drip of my own blood!

(A sound is heard, like the beating of wings of great birds)

BIRD CRIES

Is he coming, Boyg?

THE VOICE

Slowly through the mist.

BIRD CRIES

Sisters, far and wide, come to our tryst!

PEER

If you'd save me, lass, come with a rush,
Gaze not down now, never mind to blush;
Throw your Bible in his face, quickly!

BIRD CRIES

He's falling!

THE VOICE

We have him!

BIRD CRIES

Sisters, the tryst!

PEER

Dear is the price man pays for his life,
In such a tumultuous hour of strife! *(Sinks)*

BIRD CRIES

He's down! Seize him, Boyg! Into the abyss!

(Church bells and the singing of sacred music is heard in the distance.)

THE VOICE

(With a gasp he sinks to nothing.)

He was too strong! A woman, my Nemesis!

SCENE VIII

Sunrise. Mountainside in front of Ase's hut. The door is shut
—all is quiet and deserted. Peer lies asleep on a wall bunker.

PEER GYNT
(Wakes and looks about him, dull and sleepy-eyed. Spits.)
I'd give my right arm for a herring! *(Spits)*
           (Sees Helga approaching with a basket.)
Looking for someone?

HELGA
For Solveig—

PEER
(jumps up)
           Where?

HELGA
                                   Close by.

SOLVEIG
(unseen)
Stop, or I'll be going!

PEER
(stops)
'Fraid I'd hug you on the sly?

SOLVEIG
For shame!

PEER
Do you know where I was last night?
The Troll-queen is after me!

SOLVEIG
That's why we rang the bells.

PEER
I'm not the lad to be won by cow-bells.
What do you say?

HELGA
(crying)
O, she's going for good!
(runs after her)
Wait!

PEER
(catching her by the arm)
Look, sweetheart, see what I have here,
A silver button for you—speak for Peer.
Here take it!

HELGA
Let me go! Here's a basket of food.

PEER
You'd better take it or—

HELGA
Let me go! You look a fright!

PEER
(softly, letting her go)
Don't get scared—bid sister not to forget Peer!

ACT III

SCENE I

In the middle of a pine forest. A partly cloudy day in autumn, with snow flurries.

PEER GYNT
(In shirtsleeves, looks up at a giant pine, then with a terrific swing plants his axe in the tree. Stepping back, exclaims:)

Ah! Like a ruddy knight mantled in green
You stand ready for a joust, clad in steel;
So tall and stalwart, Sir Knight, I imagine
You're more becoming for a mast or keel,
But Knight Peer needs you for his own palace,
So, down you come, without ado or grace!
(Chopping)

O pshaw! It's only an ancient tree;
Shortly, noble Knight you shall bend your knee—
The bigger they are, the harder they fall—
You're not so tough or steel-armored at all!
But this woodman's task is no child's play;
It's the devil's own work when you while away
Your time in chopping and idle dreaming;
But all this must stop—dreaming and lying,
Floating on clouds, building Castles in Spain—
Now, you're friendless, an outcast, that's certain!
(chopping faster)

You're an outlaw! Now you have no mother
To bring you food or to wait upon you, Peer,
If you want to eat, you must forage for food,
From the woods and from the stream; aye, would
You have warm clothes you must skin the deer;

Split fir-roots for a fire, split logs for timber,
Cleave stones for walls, and shoulder them all there!
(Steps and gazes ahead of him)

I'll build a masterpiece! Weathervane
And tower shall rise above the roof-tree,
And on the gable I'll carve a mermaid,
With grinning gargoyles here and there,
I'll get brass for all the doors and the vane;
Each casement shall be so high and fair
That strangers, passing along, wonder-staid,
Shall ask—what's that a-glittering so adorably?
(Laughing scornfully)

More devil's lies—there I go again,
Always building more Castles in Spain!
You're homeless, friendless, an outlaw!
(Chopping vigorously)

                        A low
Thatched hut will keep out the cold and rain;
Under the circumstances, it'll do for now!
(Looking up at tree)

He quivers, he totters—one more stroke, now!
He's down! his wondrous weight makes the ground quake
And the undergrowth beneath begins to shake!

*(Begins lopping off branches, stops, listens, stands still with
uplifted axe.)*
Someone's behind me! Is that you, Hegstad,
You old gaffer? He's still on my track!
(He hides behind the tree-stump and peers out.)
Ah, it's only a lone lad—he's stopping;
Now he looks around, what is he hiding
In his coat? A sickle—with a shiver
He lays his hand flat on a fence-railing.
What's he doing? he hesitates—a thump!
Good heavens! he's chopped off a finger!
He wraps a rag about the bleeding stump!
Now he takes to his heels!

(Rising)
He's maimed for life!
Yet he did it so timidly and carefully.
Sure—that's one way to get out of the army.
But to sever a member off with a knife—
To think, to wish it done, yes, even the will—
But really to do it—that gives me a chill!

(Shakes his head, resumes chopping)

SCENE II

A room in Ase's house. Everything is in disorder — the clothescloset is open, and the clothes are scattered about; a cat's lying on the bed. Ase and Kari are busily putting the room in order and sorting things that were left.

ASE
(Running across the room.)
Kari, come here!

KARI
What is it?

ASE
Tell me—
Where did I lay—? I am looking—!
Where did I put—? Now, what did I do?
I'm out of my wits! Where's the chest key?

KARI
In the key hole!

ASE
What is that rumbling?

KARI
That's the last load they're taking to Hegstad.

ASE
(weeping)
O would to God they carried me out instead!

And He alone knows what I have been through!
God have mercy! They have stripped my house bare!
What Hegstad left, the bailiff impounded.
Even the clothes on my back were seized!
Fie! Justice feasts while I weep—'tis unfair!

(Sitting on edge of bed)

The house and furnishings are gone forever!
Old Hegstad was hard, but the Law was harder;
No one helped me or showed any mercy;
Peer has gone, and not a soul to guide me!

KARI

You can live here until you die.

ASE

Yes, I know, you would have the cat and I
Live on Charity—

KARI

Peer has cost you dear!

ASE

Never mind! don't worry about my Peer!
Ingrid came back safe and sound from her flight.
The devil's the sole source of my boy's plight,
For he alone could tempt, lead my son astray!

KARI

Had I not better send for the pastor, Ase?
You look so weak and pale in the face.

ASE

For the pastor? Perhaps you are right, Kari.

(Arising)

Not yet—I can't, even if it means my death!
He's still my son—it's a mother's duty!
I must help him, though friends have forsaken me!
Ah, here's his coat, I must mend it right away,
And there's a fur rug—I'll keep it if I may.
Now, where's his hose?

KARI

In the rubbish there, underneath.

ASE
(rummaging)

Look, what I found! An old casting ladle
With which he used to play button-molder,
And melt and pour, form and stamp them in style.
One day when John Gynt was giving a banquet
And was in his cups, and full of aquavit,
Peer came in and asked his father for some tin.
"Poof!" said his father. "We Gynts have no tin,
Here, take this gold sovereign!" His father,
Blear-eyed, couldn't tell silver from gold!
Here are the hose—all full of holes and old.
They need darning—

KARI

They certainly do!

ASE

As soon as I mend them, I'll go to bed.
I'm getting short of breath. But look! here's two *(joyfully)*
Woolen shirts that they have overlooked!
That was a lucky find—put one, Kari,
With his coat—no, we'll keep them both for a token,
The one he has on is worn and so thin!

KARI

I pray, Mother Ase, that would be a sin!

ASE

But there's no need for praying, Kari,
When you have no sins to be forgiven!

SCENE III

*At dusk in front of a newly built hut in the forest, with
reindeer horns above the door. Deep snow. Peer Gynt fastens
a large wooden bar to the front door.*

PEER GYNT
(laughing)

This bar will keep out the mischievous nixies,

And the trolls, and the malicious fairies.
In the gloaming I can hear the culprits singing—
> When the night falls
> Through nails and walls,
>> We'll come from our hiding place;
> Down the chimney we'll softly creep,
> While you snore in your sleep;
> We'll pinch your nose, tickle your toes,
> And steal anon your bed-clothes,
>> Dancing about the fireplace;
> Then swift with the wind, we'll merrily go,
> Trippingly with a Hi! and a Ho! Ho!

(Solveig, with a hood on her head and a bundle in her hand, comes on snow-shoes over the heath.)

SOLVEIG

God bless your place! You must not refuse me!
I got your message; I have come to stay!

PEER

Solveig? Impossible! Is it you, really?
Then you're not afraid now to come to me!

SOLVEIG

One message you sent by little sister,
Others came in storm and stress. But the day
I met your mother, gave courage to me,
And I owe her a debt, I hope to repay.
In those dreary and lonely nights I dreamed
I heard you, saw you, and I had to come;
I couldn't stand the loneliness any longer;
I couldn't laugh or cry, and home was not home;
I wasn't sure of you and you of me, it seemed,
But my poor little heart told me that I must come!

PEER

Your father?

SOLVEIG

I'm an orphan for the time being.
I have neither father nor mother—
I left them behind.

PEER

Solveig, my darling!
You have come to me!

SOLVEIG

Yes, to you alone.
You're my all-in-all—I turn to you for comfort,
But the worst was leaving my little sister.
Worse than that was bidding my father good-bye,
And the worst of all was to forsake my mother—
I thought my heart would break. With a sigh
I left my dear ones with some effort;
God forgive me! What is done, is done!

PEER

Did you know I'm banished from my home?
I've lost everything, even my heritage!

SOLVEIG

Much more, much more has been my sacrifice—
I, too, gave up everything in my pilgrimage!

PEER

Do you know that I am a prisoner, and a prey
To every man in the forest?

SOLVEIG

On my way
Here I was often stopped on the snow and ice—
"Whither bound?" and I only said "I'm going home."

PEER

In that case I'll need no bolts or bars,
No danger now from devilkin talk or fear!
My hunter's hut shall be free from all jars.
O let me look at you! But not too near!
Just to look at you! My, you're sweet and charming!
Let me lift you! so delicate and light,
And I'll never tire in carrying you, dear.
Who'd believe you'd come to me tonight!
But I have yearned for you, my darling.
Look, I've built this cabin for my little runaway!
I'll build a new one, more beautiful, some day!

SOLVEIG

Let it be grand or ever so humble, Peer,
Here the air is so pure and invigorating;
At home it was like a tomb—suffocating
And offensive—that's one reason why I came;
I like the open forest, the wild game,
The murmuring pines, where all is quiet and fair,
Amid the sweet songs of birds—I'm at home here.

PEER

But dear, are you sure? This means forever!

SOLVEIG

There's no turning back now!

PEER

What could be sweeter?
Go in, sweetheart, I shall gather some firewood;
Go in, sit by the fire, take off your hood,
We'll chat together in the fire's flickering shadows.

*(He unbars the door; Solveig goes in. He stands still for
awhile, then with a loud laugh he leaps into the air for joy.)*

My princess! I have found her and won her!
We'll build a palace together—who knows!

*(He seizes his axe and moves into the woods; at the same
time an Old Woman, in a tattered green dress, comes out of
the woods; an ugly brat, with an ale-flagon in his hand, limps
after her, holding onto her skirt.)*

THE WOMAN

Good evening, Peer Lightfoot!

PEER

What? Who's there?

THE WOMAN

An old friend, Peer Gynt. My hut is quite near,
We're neighbors.

PEER

Really? That's wonderful!

THE WOMAN

As your hut was builded, mine was built, too.

PEER

I must go—

THE WOMAN

Always on the go, so artful!

But I'm right at your heels, I'll catch up to you!

PEER

You're mistaken, mother!

THE WOMAN

I know, once before,

When you promised to make me your queen—

PEER

I promised? I don't understand your behavior!

THE WOMAN

Have you forgotten the time you drank with my father?

O, don't you recall, Peer, the lass in green?

PEER

I've forgotten what I have never known or seen.

Nonsense—when did I ever meet your father?

THE WOMAN

When last we met was when first we met.

(To the Brat—)

Give your father a drink. He's thirsty, my pet!

PEER

Father? You're drunk, woman! Do you mean this imp?

THE WOMAN

Can't you tell the pig by the color of his skin?

Can't you see? Can't you see that he has a limp

In his leg as you are lame in your mind?

PEER

You imagine!—

THE WOMAN

Doesn't he look like some of your kin?

PEER

This leering, long-legged—

THE WOMAN
He grows like the wind.

PEER

Why, you pig-woman!

THE WOMAN
You're as uncouth as an ox!
True, I've lost my beauty, my golden locks,
Since you lured me up there on the hill;
In my travail I had only the devil
To help me. But to see me fair as before
You've only to turn that wench from your door;
Drive her out of your mind and out of sight,
And you'll see me, Peer, in a different light!

PEER

On your way, old sow!

THE WOMAN
I'll do nothing of the kind!

PEER

I'll chop off your head with my axe.

THE WOMAN
You talk to the wind!
Try if you dare, Peer Gynt. I have no fear!
I'll spy on you both, I'll peep through the chinks
In the walls; I'll peer through the windows and the door
When you spoon and cuddle on the hearth-floor;
I'll be there, too, at the wrong time like a jinx.
O what a lovely triangle with Peer as Lothario,
Good-bye, Peer, you can marry her tomorrow!

PEER

Avaunt, she-devil!

THE WOMAN
By the way, take devilkin,
Your son, you ignis fatuus, home to your kin;
Take care of him! Will you go to your dad, my brat?

THE BRAT
(Spitting on him)
Rats! I'd like to hit him on the head with a bat!

THE WOMAN
(Kissing the brat)
What a head, what shoulders, has little castaway!
O Peer, he'll be a chip off the old block some day!

PEER
(Kicking the ground)
I wish I was as far—

THE WOMAN
As now as we are near!

PEER
(Clenching his fist)
And all this comes—

THE WOMAN
From trespassing, and insincere
Promises! Too bad! Swiftfoot!

PEER
But it's so cruel
To her, Solveig, my sweetheart, my jewel!

THE WOMAN
Aye, the guiltless, too, must smart, said the Devil—
As a mother beat her son when father stunk like a still!
(She goes on with the Brat, who throws the flagon at Peer.)

PEER
(After a long pause)
Go roundabout, said the Boyg, and that's no jest,
Down goes my palace, down goes my love-nest!
But there's a wall between us now, alas!
All my joy and love and hope have gone to grass!
Roundabout, Peer, take the devious way—
There's no straight path to my true love, I'd say.
Right through? Surely there must be a right way.
Somewhere in the Scriptures, I remember,

It speaks about repentance. I've no book,
I've forgotten, and I wouldn't know where to look!
Besides there's no one to guide me—no preacher
In these pathless woods. Repent? It'll take years
To pick up the loose ends, and allay my fears—
You can mend a violin but never a ball;
Trample the cushioned moss with your heel,
And it gives you a bit of a heartache. But surely
The old pig-woman was lying to me!
I'll put all foolishness and lying out of sight;
But can I put them out of mind—outright,
Or shall I be haunted by lurking memories
Of Ingrid, the cow-herd maidens, the troll girlies?
Must I lift them up and hold them out at arm's length?
Go roundabout! It's no use, Peer! Had I the strength
And reach of the pine-trees' branches, I'd hold her
Too close to set her down unsullied! Moreover,
I stand to gain nothing, to lose nothing!
Go roundabout, Peer! Repent and stop lying!

(Starts towards the hut)

Go in after this, Peer? Smelling of swill!
Besides all the Troll-folks are hunting me still!
Speak, but be silent—confess, but conceal!

(Throwing away his axe)

It's Sunday evening, to go into the cottage,
Such as I am now, would be sacrilege!

SOLVEIG

Are you coming?

PEER
(softly)
Roundabout!

SOLVEIG
What?

PEER
You must wait!
I've got something to carry in, and it's late!

SOLVEIG

Wait, Peer, I will help you! I will come down!

PEER

No, stay there, I must bear it all alone!

SOLVEIG

Don't go too far, dear!

PEER

Be patient my own;
Be my way long or short—you must wait!

SOLVEIG

Yes, I shall wait!

(Peer goes down the path; Solveig remains in the doorway.)

SCENE IV

Ase's room. Evening. In the fireplace flickers a small fire; a cat sits on a stool at the foot of the bed; Ase abed, restlessly picking at the bedclothes.

ASE

Have mercy on me, dear Lord;
The nights are long and dreary.
If he'd only send me word,
Or see me before I go,
Then I could die happily.
The time is short, I should know.
Forgive my angry words, Peer—
They've cost me many a tear!

PEER GYNT

Good evening!

ASE

God be praised!
Day and night have I prayed,

But to enter the valley,
My boy, is utmost folly!

                    PEER

Don't worry about me, mother
There's nothing left but the lees.

                    ASE

Kari has gone to her saeter,
And I can depart in peace.

                    PEER

Depart? O what are you saying?
Where do you think you're going?

                    ASE

Ah, my son, my end is near—
And soon I'll be with your father, Peer.

                    PEER

I am fleeing from sorrow;
I fled from the woods and the wold—
I must leave you tomorrow.
Are your feet and hands acold?

                    ASE

Tomorrow I shall be gone—
My eyes glaze, I pick the clothes,
Don't forget my eyes to close,
Carefully and tenderly.
Get me a coffin at dawn,
A goodly one for to see.

                    PEER

O rest, rest your weary soul,
Mother, and don't be so droll.

                    ASE
               (looking restlessly around)
The Law took most everything,
Aye, even down to my wedding ring.

                    PEER

Tut, tut, there you go again;
But you have right to complain.

ASE

No! it's that accursed drink
That has brought you to the brink!
Ah, my boy, when you're drinking
You never know what you're doing.
For you were riding the deer—
No wonder you acted so queer!

PEER

Let's forget the past, mother—
'Tis water under the bridge.
Let's talk of something better
While the moon peers o'er the ridge.

(Sitting on edge of the bed.)

Let's harp and carp a wee bit;
Forget the tedious nights,
Wanton burdens we'll omit,
And talk of sweeter delights.
Look at Old Puss on the chair—
She has a peculiar air.

ASE

At night she'll moan and growl
As if she'd lost some poor soul.

PEER
(Changing the subject.)
What news? What news from the valley?

ASE
(smiling)

It's noised about freely
There's a girl with golden locks—

PEER
(hastily)
How's Mads, the fat-faced ox?

ASE

Kari says she's run away
And her folks just pray and pray.

PEER

But what does the smithy say?

ASE

Don't talk of that crazy churl!
He has now another girl.
Ah, but goldie-locks is a pearl!—

PEER

Let's harp and carp a wee bit,
Forget the tedious nights,
Wanton burdens we'll omit,
And talk of sweeter delights.
O let me bring you a drink.
Can you stretch? Have you a kink
Or a stitch in your left side?
The bed's short and not too wide—
Bless me! my own trundle-bed!
Many a time and oft you've spread
The fur coverlet o'er me,
And told me many a story.

ASE

Ah yes, we'd play the bed a sleigh
When your father was abroad;
The floor was the icy fjord,
And the bedspread our sleigh-robe—
Ah, once we had a fine robe!

PEER

But the best of all, of course,
Mother, was our prancing horse!

ASE

Yes, I know—'twas Kari's cat
We borrowed. Ha! ha! it sat
On the stool at the foot of the bed,
Ah, yes, and how she purred!

PEER

The Castle West of the Moon,
The Castle East of the Sun,

To Soria-Moria Castle—
The sun and moon are changing shifts,
And the balm of the poppy drifts
Softly over the valley.
A stick we found in the hall,
Made a good whip, I recall.

ASE

I sat in the driver's seat.

PEER

Ah, yes, you drove with loose reins,
Kept turning round and asking
If I were cold! You're so sweet,
Mother! God bless you! More pains?

ASE

Here! Here, my back is aching!

PEER

Now, I'll draw you up a bit—
There! You'll feel much better.

ASE
(Uneasily)

No, Peer, I must go—

PEER
Leaving?

ASE

Yes, Peer, I've lost my spirit—

PEER

I'll sit on the bed, mother;
Let me fix the bed-cover,
And we'll shorten the evening
With many a lusty hymn.

ASE

Bring me, Peer, the Holy Writ!
I am going to meet Him!

PEER

In Soria-Moria Castle

The King is giving a feast;
Lie back on your pillow,
I'll drive you straight to the King.
You'll be a twice welcome guest!

ASE

Guest?

PEER

Yes, we're going right now!

*(He throws a cord round the back of the chair on which the
cat is lying, and with the cane in his hand, sits down at the
foot of the bed.)*

Giddyap, giddyap, Blackie!
Do you feel cold, mother?
Wait till Blackie warms up, too,
Then we'll fly along, duckie!

ASE

What's that singing and ringing?

PEER

'Tis only sleigh-bells, mother,
You hear from over the moor.

ASE

Mercy, Peer, what's that rumbling,
So hollow and loud at the door,
Like the coming of the Lord?

PEER

Hush, dear—we're crossing the fjord!

ASE

What's that a-sighing so drear,
A-whispering in my ear?

PEER

'Tis only the fir-trees' soughing!
Be still, mother, have no fear!

ASE

Slow up—there's a gleam afar,
Shining, dancing like a star.

PEER

'Tis only the castle's glaze—
There's Old St. Peter, and prays
That you'll come directly in!

ASE

Are you sure of what he says—
Don't you know they turned Christ's kin
Away from Bethlehem Inn?

PEER

Yes! Yes! He bids you come in,
And brings you the choicest wine!

ASE

And cakes to go with the wine?

PEER

Ah, enough for a German picnic!
The vicar's wife has a cake so thick—

ASE

Lordy! Like meeting old friends!

PEER

Aye! her best wishes she extends!

ASE

My, such a show, such a whirl,
You're driving me out of this world!

PEER
(cracking his whip)

Giddyap, giddyap, Blackie!

ASE

You're sure you know the way, Peer?

PEER
(cracking the whip)

I know the way, dear, be still!

ASE

But I feel tired and ill!

PEER

The Castle's walls we have won!
And our journey's almost done!

ASE

I'll lie back and close my eyes,
And trust all to you, my boy!

PEER

Whoa! Slow up, Blackie, my boy!
They swarm the castle like flies;
Peer Gynt and his Ase are here!
What do you say, St. Peter?
You won't let in my mother!
O you can tell at a glance
Mother's such a pious soul,
Her name must be on your scroll!
For my sake, alas, it's too late,
I can turn back at the gate;
But if you will take a chance,
It's all the same to me—
I'm no angel, St. Peter;
Like St. Nick in the pulpit,
I have told my share of lies,
Called my mother an old hen—
She pecked me now and then.
Revere and respect mother,
And make her feel right at home;
She'll honor your kingdom—
You'll always be in her debt.
Ho, ho? here's your Godfather,
St. Peter, now you'll catch it. *(In a loud laugh)*
"Come off your high horse, Peter,
Now mother shall enter free."
That'll hold you for awhile, Peter!

*(Laughs loudly, goes over to window by Ase's bed. Ase slowly
raises herself upon one elbow, and looks up at the sky.)*

ASE

The Large Stars are His Sheep,
The Little Stars His Lambs,
And the Moon His Shepherd,
But where are the Blessed Dams?
Aye, they're with Him, the Lord,
And now I lay me down— —

(Sinks on pillow)

PEER

(Turning around)

Why do you stare so, mother?
Speak! Your eyes are so glassy!
Look, mother, it's I, your Peer!

(He feels her forehead, tosses the cord on the chair.)

At ease, Blackie! we've lost our driver—
Our long, long journey is o'er!

(Closes her eyelids, and bends over her.)

O thanks for all the beatings,
The kisses and the scoldings,
But you must thank me, dear!

(Presses his cheek to her mouth)

There! that was for the long ride!

KARI

(entering)

What! Peer? Her worries are over
With you here, lad, at her side!
O how soundly she's sleeping—
Or is she—

PEER

Hush, she is dead!

*(Kari weeps at Ase's head; Peer passes slowly up and down,
then places his hand on Kari's shoulder—)*

Have a fine funeral, Kari;
I must leave immediately.

                          KARI
Leaving?

                          PEER
              To sea!

                          KARI
                    So far?

                          PEER
                          Very far!

ACT IV

SCENE I

A palm-grove on the Southwest coast of Morocco. A table is spread for dinner under an awning. The floor is covered with rush matting. Farther back in the grove hammocks are hanging. Off shore a steam yacht flying the Norwegian and American flags. On the beach a jolly-boat. Sunset.

Peer Gynt, now a handsome, middle-aged man, tailored in a neat traveling suit, with a pair of gold-rimmed eyeglasses dangling from his waistcoat, presides at the head of the table. Mr. Cotton, Monsieur Ballon, Herren von Eberkopf and Trumpeterstrale are finishing dinner.

PEER GYNT

Drink up, men! If man was born for pleasure,
Then let him be sociable at all cost.
What's gone is gone, and what's lost is lost,
They say. Gentlemen, what's your pleasure?

TRUMPETERSTRALE

Brother, you're an unusual host!

PEER

I share that honor with my monies,
My cook, my steward and my cronies.

MR. COTTON

Permit me to offer you four a toast!

MONSIEUR BALLON

Monsieur, you have a *gout*, a *ton*,
Very seldom encountered now-a-days
Among men living *en garçon*—
A something—I forget the phrase.

90

EBERKOPF

A citizen of the world, who has seen
The world on either side, and who cherishes
His adopted land as his own; by nature keen,
A crafty man—*impartial, incomparable,
Serene, convivial, strong, inimitable;
Forever seeking Fame and Fortune and Friends,
His ambition and his goal never ends.
Nicht wahr, monsieur, that's what you mean?

MONSIEUR BALLON

Quite so, Mein Herr, but in my tongue
It wouldn't sound so flowery—

EBERKOPF

Ei was! Like an ear-kissing song,
But let's sift off the pros and cons, we'll see—

PEER

That's simple, gentlemen. I've no marital ties.
To look out for himself is man's first duty—
The survival of the fittest—you know the theory.
But how can you do this encumbered,
Like a pack-mule, with others' worries?

EBERKOPF

But I dare say this self-love, Mein Herr,
Has now and then cost you very dear.

PEER

Yes, indeed, in my youth, but undaunted
I've always come off with flying honor;
Once they almost caught me off my guard.
I was a handsome lad, wild, full of vigor,
And was ensnared by a lass, a royal ward—

MONSIEUR BALLON

Nobility?

PEER
(carelessly)
An old House.

TRUMPETERSTRALE
(thumping the table)
A troll, no doubt.

PEER
(wincing)
These bogus Highbrows permit no commoner to blot
Their sacred escutcheon.

MR. COTTON
You were engaged?

MONSIEUR BALLON
So?

PEER
(nonchalantly)
Yes, by royal command.
But 'twas an explicable love tangle.
The whole affair was sort of bittersweet—
I disagreed in every particular.
I'm a free-lance, like to stand on both feet,
And I took a dislike to the royal fanfare.
Her father hedged on my dowry—insisted
That I must change my name, be glorified
In a new coat-of-arms. In vain I tried
To reason with him; I lost my head,
I cared naught for the throne or title;
Eventually, I renounced my charming bride.
(Drumming on the table with a pious air)
Allons, monsieur, Destiny's magic wand
Comforts and guides us on every hand!

MONSIEUR BALLON
And thus ended your romance?

PEER
No, not quite.
I'll never forget that auspicious night—
Some insidious courtiers, gulled by my crime,
Frowned, foamed, fumed, and began the strife,
While some unbidden guests, put up a fight.

I fought seven of them at one time,
And vanquished them, one by one, in the duel;
I lost some blood, but that bloody battle
Again attests that I bear a charmed life!

EBERKOPF

You're an uncanny philosopher, that's certain,
But with all your philosophy, still a man;
The average thinker sees everything in due form,
But cannot distinguish the chaff from the grain.
Herr Peer sees everything with minute perspective—
His perceptions so ether-like, so volatile,
Converge eventually to a common norm,
Fathoming every fallacy at every turn!
No schooling? All this sounds superhuman!

PEER

I am a self-made man and self-taught,
I've never learned by rote, but always sought
To keep informed on every useful subject.
You see, I started late in life, my prospect
Was not rosy, and my handicaps were many.
History I found a pageant, philosophy, pendantic;
Of religion I had only a smattering;
But experience is an education in itself—
Hit and miss, give and take, day by day,
One soon learns to master things the hard way,
To pursue the expedient and adjust himself.
Yes, friends, I came from the School of Hardknocks.
I now peruse my books and count my stocks,
And I hope to graduate *cum laude* like a King!

MR. COTTON

Very practical, Mr. Peer, I dare say!

PEER
(lighting a cigar)

As I said before, I'm a self-made man;
I started from scratch, on a shoestring;
Many a time I walked the streets without a dime.
Life, my friends, is dear, and death has its sting.

My father was an eminent merchantman.
He won and lost a dozen fortunes in his prime.
His pedlar's pack is a priceless heirloom.
Such is the sturdy stock from which I spring.
Fate, and Luck, too, has been a faithful groom,
And Prosperity brought me a multitude of friends.
They called me Croesus of the Carolinas;
My argosies of sails haunted the Seven Seas,
Bringing me rare cargoes and rich dividends!

MR. COTTON
What did you trade in?

PEER
Like a buccaneer
I sold slaves to Carolina and idols to China!

MONSIEUR BALLON
Fi donc!

TRUMPETERSTRALE
The devil, Uncle Peer!

PEER
But, gentlemen, I've always kept within the law,
Even if my enterprises were a little shady—
I like to play the game according to Hoyle,
But, the great humanitarian that I am, I foresaw
The capriciousness of public taste and favor.
Yes, I would liquidate, yet I couldn't endure
The thought of losing my workers and my far-flung
Empire. I was ageing, slowly but surely,
My hair was thinning and turning gray, too.
I finally succumbed to the teachings of Sing Sang Sung,
The great Chinese philosopher, who admonishes
"It's later than you think—you can't take it with you."
I decided, my friends, to turn over a new leaf;
In the spring I sent shiploads of heathen idols;
In the fall, I followed them up with missionaries
To convert them, supplying the wandering apostles
With clothing, food, rice and rum, and bibles!

MR. COTTON

And, with a profit, I presume?

PEER

        The plan paid well, brother.
Everything, as you all know, has its own price—
With every idol we gave a sack of rice;
In no time the missionaries were working in shifts,
Converting, baptizing—one thing offsets the other;
We were repaid double for our trouble and gifts!

MR. COTTON

How about your slave trade? Do you supply—

PEER

My ethics—my conscience, got the upper hand.
I was getting too old to trade in contraband;
At my age you never know when your time is nigh,
And there were a thousand more pitfalls
Laid by the false prophets, my so-called friends,
Pirates, zealots, revenue agents, the elements;
Pull in your sails, I said, and make amends.
Why work in the devil's smithy? Pooh, you say!
I bought in the Carolinas a large plantation;
In the sunny South I settled my last importation.
It worked, and soon grew prosperous and happy,
And this made me the happiest of men.
I built them stores, schools and cathedrals.
I soon retired, sold the plantation,
Gave them a farewell celebration—
So rare with the Mason and Dixon planters.
Complete and genuine was my reformation.
He who does no ill, does good, says the Orient,
So I put my house in order, gentlemen,
Hoping my sins are offset by my charity.

EBERKOPF

(clinking glasses with him)

How gratifying it is to have a principle
So adroitly worked out, so singularly freed
From the ambiguities of theory—

PEER
(slightly intoxicated)

In my country we understand the need
Of preparation for defense. Our homely creed
Is simple—Look out for the snake in the grass!

MR. COTTON

What sort of a snake, my dear friend?

PEER
(drinking)

One that slyly tempts man to make a false pass.
A brave man can move on without fear, and extend
His lines safely without ambush or surprise.
He, however, never burns the bridges behind him
Until he has won his objective without compromise.
This homespun creed has always been my maxim!

MONSIEUR BALLON

You're Norwegian?

PEER

By birth, yes; in spirit
I am a citizen of the world. In America
I made my fortune. From modern Germany
I furnished my library. From France my piquancy
For dress. From England my manners and wit
And bull-dog tenacity. The Jew taught me patience.
My taste for *dolce far niente* from Italy.
In my youth, in many a perilous strife,
Cold, cold Swedish steel oft has saved my life!

TRUMPETERSTRALE
(lifting his glass)

Aye, to Swedish steel—there's none better!

EBERKOPF

Let's drink to the dauntless cavalier!
(They clink their glasses while Peer becomes more garrulous)

MR. COTTON

But, my dear sir, you say you are getting old.
Tell us what you intend to do with your gold!

PEER

(smiling)

My plan, you ask?

ALL FOUR

(surrounding him)

We would like to hear!

PEER

Well, first of all, I intend to travel;
I invited you aboard my yacht for company
At Gibraltar to enliven the dull nights and quaff
My champagne, and dance around my Golden Calf.

EBERKOPF

Very witty!

MR. COTTON

We know some sail the Mediterranean
For pleasure; but a trader like you, my good man,
Must have some profitable object in mind—

PEER

To be Emperor!

ALL FOUR

What!

PEER

(nodding)

To rule mankind!

ALL FOUR

Where?

PEER

Of the whole world!

MONSIEUR BALLON

But how, friend?

PEER

Simple, gentlemen—by the might of my gold.
The scheme, you know, is very, very old,
But it has always been my life's ambition.

Even as a lad I built Castles in Spain,
Soared through the clouds, over sea and mountain
With my mantle, crown and gilded scabbard,
Then fell down on all fours in humiliation.
I don't remember where, but somewhere 'tis said—
What profits a man if he gains the world
Only to lose himself in life's giddy whirl.
What you gain is but a garland on a dead man's head—
Only a throne I crave, not a wreath or a grave!

EBERKOPF

But what, then, is the Gyntish Self, brother?

PEER

The world behind my brow, Myself, no other!
I—I that I am—no more than God's the devil!

TRUMPETERSTRALE

Why, of course!

MONSIEUR BALLON

A thinker!

EBERKOPF

So versatile!

PEER

The Gyntish Self is the best, take my word—
Of longings, hopes, ambitions and desires.
The Gyntish Self—a sea of fancies, fears, pleasures,
And all that which makes every man's heart beat bold.
Yet, as God hallows the dust to proclaim him Lord
Of the world, I am not deaf to the sweet measures
Of the music that comes from the clink, clink of gold!
(tapping the decanter with the rim of his glasses)
If I'm to become the Emperor of the World!

MONSIEUR BALLON

Well now, it seems, your coffers are plumb full—

PEER

Pooh! To spend only a week-end at Lippe takes
A small fortune, gentlemen! I—Sir Peter Gynt

Require more gold! I aspire for higher stakes,
But I must be Myself *en bloc,* aye—powerful,
To rule the whole world—each state a Gynt-mint!

MONSIEUR BALLON
(enraptured)

To possess all the beauty the world can offer!

EBERKOPF

To buy up all the bins of Johannesberger!

TRUMPETERSTRALE

And all the spurs of Charles the Twelfth at Bender!

MR. COTTON

A seat on the Board of Trade!

PEER
                    Then lend me your ear,
My lord—that's why we're anchored here.
Tonight we sail to the other end of the Mere.
I've just received word of the greatest importance.
Now is the time to woo Fortune with diligence!

ALL FOUR

Go on, tell us quickly!

PEER
                    Greece has revolted!

ALL FOUR
(springing up)

What! Greece?

PEER
Yes, their borders are closed!

ALL FOUR

Hurrah!

PEER
The Turks have been attacked!

MONSIEUR BALLON

To arms—let Glory's banners advance!
I'll help them with the sword of France!

EBERKOPF
I'll lend them my voice—at a distance!

MR. COTTON
And I'll supply them with English steel!

TRUMPETERSTRALE
Lead on! At Bender-abbas I'll find the gear
Charles the Twelfth left behind—I swear!

MONSIEUR BALLON
(falling on Peer's neck)
Forgive me, Sir Gynt, if I've been uncivil!

EBERKOPF
(pressing his hands)
And I mistook you for a scoundrel!

MR. COTTON
That's too strong, rather I say—a yokel!

TRUMPETERSTRALE
(embracing Peer)
And I took you for a Yankee gold-digger!

EBERKOPF
(trying to kiss him)
Now, all that has been exploded—our error!

PEER
What's all this idle talk?

EBERKOPF
We now see the glory—
The bright banners of Sir Peter Gynt's army
Of wishes, aspirations, desires, *und so weiter!*

MONSIEUR BALLON
(admiringly)
Ah!—so *this* is being Monsieur Gynt!

EBERKOPF
Ja, ja, mein Herr, ich bin nur ein Kind!

PEER

But tell me, gentlemen—

MONSIEUR BALLON

Why, don't you see?

PEER

I can't make head or tail out of your discourse!

MONSIEUR BALLON

You will furnish the Greeks with guns and money!

PEER

(with a sneer)

O no! I always bet on the best horse!

MONSIEUR BALLON

Impossible!

EBERKOPF

You must have your joke, my lordship!

PEER

*(After a pause, leans on a chair, takes a drink, and assumes a
dignified air)*

Listen, gentlemen, I think we'd better quit
Before the last vestige of our friendship
Goes up in smoke. They say, he who has nothing
Can always take a long chance, but he who has
No more than his shadow, at his best, is fit
Only for common cannon-fodder; whereas
A man like me—Sir Peter Gynt—who has everything,
His risk and his stakes, is even greater.
Go to Greece at once! I'll put you ashore at night,
And furnish you free all the arms you require.
Strike home, comrades, for Freedom and for Right!
The more you fan the flames of strife, the better;
Give the barbarians hell, give them no quarter;
Make Peter or Paul, or both, pay—I should care!
But, excuse me—I'm your silent partner,
I have all the necessary gold—right here!

(slaps his pocket)

And I am ever Myself—Sir Peter Gynt!

*(Raises his umbrella and goes out into the grove where the
hammocks are hanging.)*

TRUMPETERSTRALE

The swinish cur!

MONSIEUR BALLON

No taste for honor, the skin-flint!

MR. COTTON

Or glory—that's another story. What a gold mine
If we could free Greece from Turkish power!

MONSIEUR BALLON

I saw myself crowned the man of the hour,
Surrounded by Grecian women and wine!

TRUMPETERSTRALE

And to think I was about to drink a toast
To those famous spurs Charles the Twelfth lost!

EBERKOPF

And I saw the Kultur of my beloved fatherland
Spread far and wide over the sea and land!

MR. COTTON

There goes my fondest dream over the dam!
And such a rich, productive land! God-damn!
I saw myself sitting atop of Old Olympus,
Whose venerable veins abound in copper ore,
And whose waterfalls, so precipitous
Could easily furnish a million horsepower.

TRUMPETERSTRALE

Still, I shall go! My Swedish sword shall uphold
My honor—the devil take his unsavory gold!

MR. COTTON

Perhaps. But fighting in the common ranks,
Gentlemen, is not to my liking. No thanks,
There's no profit in that!

MONSIEUR BALLON

So near to our goal
And now left stranded on a foreign shoal!

MR. COTTON
(shaking fist at yacht)
And to think, alas, in those golden coffers
Lies a fortune sweated out of those poor niggers!

EBERKOPF
A splendid idea! His empire is a prize!
The Gyntish Self! A sight for sore eyes!

MONSIEUR BALLON
What would you do?

EBERKOPF
Seize his yacht, his power!
Buy off the crew. We can steam out in an hour!

MR. COTTON
You'll do what?

EBERKOPF
(going down to the jolly)
We'll take over! Come, grab an oar!

MR. COTTON
(following)
It stinks—but count me in!

TRUMPETERSTRALE
Such villainy!

MONSIEUR BALLON
A rascal, but *en fin!*
(follows)

TRUMPETERSTRALE
(follows the others)
Well, beggars can't be choosers!

SCENE II

*Another part of the coast. Moonlight. Drifting clouds. The
yacht now far out at sea, is steaming at full speed. Peer Gynt
it running fanatically along the shore, now pinching his arms,
now gazing out to sea.*

PEER GYNT

A nightmare. My brain's in a whirl! I'm dreaming!
She's going at full speed! Heading out to sea!
Is it a dream, or am I drunk, or plumb crazy?
(wringing his hands)
Impossible, God, that I should perish this way!
(tearing his hair)
A dream—that's it—it must be so—I'm dreaming!
Horrible! But unfortunately it is true!
My friends, the beasts! O my God, do you hear me?
O God you're wise and just—do something I pray!
(with upstretched arms)
It is I—I, Peter Gynt! Do not delay!
Run upon the sea, Father, you've done it before!
Stop the robbers! O blow up the boilers some way!
What a mess! Don't forsake me, Lord, one more favor!
Let the world take care of itself for awhile!
No, he hears me not—he is deaf as usual!
(beckons upwards)
Perhaps indisposed—my case is too trivial!
Hist! I've given the nigger plantations away,
And flooded China with missionaries, Father.
Surely one good turn deserves another!

*(An explosion is heard in the offing, fire shoots from the
yacht, followed by thick clouds of smoke. Peer Gynt, pale
and thunderstruck, sinks to the beach with a shriek. When
the smoke clears away the ship has vanished.)*

Dreadful is the wrath of the Lord! All hands struck
In a moment! God be praised! It was my good luck

Not to be there. It's more than that—it's Providence!
Thanks to Him, my protector. 'Tis evidence
He keeps an eye on me in spite of my failings.
What a fine feeling of comfort and safety
To know that you're guarded constantly!
Yet, in this desert, where'll I find food or shelter?
I'll leave that to Him! I'm sure there's no danger!
                    (brashly)
He'd never let a little sparrow like me famish!
Be humble—give the Lord time, don't be selfish,
Don't get down-hearted, and don't forget his blessings.
What was that? Sounded like a lion in the bushes.
                    (his teeth chatter)
Can't be a lion!
                    (Plucking up courage)
                    The King of King's not that foolish
To tangle with the Lord! Let him think of my yacht!
Their instinct, of course, tells them what's what!
Now I only need shelter—I must find a tree.
Over there is a grove of acacias and palms.
Here I'll take my stand and sing a few psalms.
                    (climbing up tree)
Morning and evening are never the same, they say.
Here the air is pleasant and most peaceful.
                    (seating himself comfortably)
To think nobly is worth more than great riches.
He knows, too, when my cup of affliction is full,
And treats me like a son in every way.
(Sighs, looks to the sea where his ship blew up, then whispers)
But He's not economical, as you can see!

SCENE III

Moroccan soldiers bivouac on the edge of the desert about a watchfire.

A SLAVE
(enters, tearing his hair)
The Emperor's spotless charger is gone!

ANOTHER SLAVE
(enters, rending his garments)
They've stolen the Emperor's sacred gown!

AN OFFICER
(enters)
In the name of Allah, up with you nit-wits!
Scour the desert, seek out the culprits!
Or I'll flog you swine, one by one!

SCENE IV

*Dawn. A clump of acacias and palms. Peer Gynt, in a tree,
is trying to ward off a swarm of monkeys with a branch.*

PEER GYNT

Confound it! A most disagreeable night!
(Swats around him)
Now they toss nuts, now make faces—what a sight!
I think the ape is the orneriest beast of all!
Watch and wait—I'm so tired, I'm afraid I'll fall.
I must get one of these imps and skin him alive.
I'll trade places, I'll beat them at their own game.
We mortals don't vary much, wild or tame.
Here they come again—how they jump and dive!
Scat! Shoo! If I only had my flashy troll-tail,
They might make up to me, but that orange bow
Would make them jealous. Ho! Grandma's going to throw!

*(Crouches, keeps still for awhile. The ape moves, Peer tries
to coax the ape like a dog)*

Hi there, Fanny! So friendly now she makes faces;
She'll listen to reason, she has sense, now she braces—
No, she'll not throw, will you doggie? We're friends!
Woof! woof! we can talk. You see she comprehends.
Why you dirty slut! Right on my pate! you're no lady!
But it doesn't even taste like food—not a bit!
I thought they'd show some hospitality!
And the little rascals don't vary a whit;
Like kids they must show off before company!
(Swatting about)
It's a shame that man, the lord of creation,
Should have to suffer hell and damnation!

SCENE V

*Early morning. A stony region overlooking the desert. On
one side a cleft in the hill and a cave. A Thief and a Receiver of stolen goods in the cleft with the Emperor's horse
and robes. The horse, richly caparisoned, is tethered to a
rock. Horsemen in the distance.*

THIEF

Hark! I hear troopers coming,
Their pennons proudly gleaming
  In the morning breeze.

RECEIVER

Fly! I see my head swinging
  From the desert trees.

THIEF

(folding arms on breast)

My poor father was a thief,
  And steal must I.

RECEIVER

And my father was a Fence,
  And so am I.

THIEF

Let us bear our lot and grief—
  Trust to Providence!

RECEIVER

(listening)

Silence! Footsteps I can hear!
  Away man! But where?

THIEF

Yonder cave is deep and long—
  Allah's good and strong!

*(They flee and leave their booty behind. The horsemen disap-
pear in the distance.)*

PEER GYNT
(whittling a reed whistle)

What a glorious morning! In the sand sweeps
The beetle rolling his ball. From his shell peeps
The snail. Dawn now comes on with golden hands,
Refreshing the air like a thousand garlands,
So invigorating, one feels so safe and bold.
Such solitude! The joys of Nature unfold!
Inconceivable—much have I missed till now.
Pity the gulled man in the city—I know!
Aye, look at those lizards frisking about!
O what a care-free life these beasts eke out!
The Lord put them here for a purpose, no doubt—
They work and fight to preserve their species.

(Puts on his eyeglasses)

Ha, a toad! Imprisoned in a rock! He's all eyes!
Leering at the world from his cell—he's himself, enough!

(musing)

Enough—to himself? I've heard that before—old stuff—
But where? My memory fails me now and then.

(Reclining in the shade)

Here it's cool and restful—I'll stretch on the green,
And there's ferns growing with edible roots between.

(Tasting one)

'Tis food fit only for beasts, but then they say
Curb your Nature—and—The proud shall fall by the way.
Again—Whoso humbleth himself shall be exalted.
Exalted! That's been my life's ambition!
Friend Fate will take care of me—I'll be saved
As usual, and put on the road to wealth!
'Tis but a trial, my rescue is good as begun!
If only He will allow me to keep my health!

*(Nonchalantly lights a cigar, stretches his legs, and gazes out
over the desert.)*

O, what an endless, boundless desert!
And what did God really mean when He created
This desert, bereft of all usefulness;
This sprawling, burnt-out cinder, this inert

Fragment, this enigma of nothingness,
This corpse which has never even breathed,
Nor reimbursed the Creator for His trouble!
O, how careless is Nature—'tis unbelievable!
Is that the sea that glistens in the east?
No, 'tis only a mirage. The sea's to the west,
Dammed out by the shelving sands. A dam?
That's it! The hills are low. Very feasible.
Dig a ditch, a canal, that'll do it easily!
'Twould be a lifesaver for this desolate spot—
Each oasis would become a bustling island-grot.
On the north, Atlas would lift his great shoulders;
On the south, ships bound for the East, like gossamers,
Would dispense the caravan's packs far and wide;
Life-giving breezes would refresh the countryside;
From the clouds gentle showers with every breeze,
And grass growing round the thirsty palm-trees;
Town after town shall arise in the south
Behind Sahara's wall, once naught but drouth.
Seaports, villages and cities shall sprout
Like mushrooms; new colonies for Bornu;
Steam shall drive the factories at Timbuctu,
And the explorer, without going roundabout,
Can reach the Upper Nile. In the midst of the sea,
On a rich oasis, I'll settle my Norsemen,
For Dalesmen's blood is as good as royalty;
I'll cross my kin with Arab blood now and then.
On a broad bay with a most charming strand,
I'll build Peeropolis, the capital and chief city.
The world's old! Give way to Gyntiana—my land!

                     (Springing up)

All I need is capital, and the job's done!
A golden key will open the gates of the sea!
A crusade against death! Aye, the scurvy churl
Shall disgorge all his holdings. The whole world
Prays for peace, freedom and equality in unison.
Like Noah's ass in the ark, I'll raise my voice,
And bray a message to the world. Let them rejoice!
I'll dedicate Gyntiana and the entire canal

To mankind! Onward, Sir Peter, find the capital!
My kingdom—well, say half of it—for a horse!
> *(The horse in the cleft neighs)*

A horse, weapons, robes, ornaments and a sword!
> *(going closer)*

Impossible! Yet it is true. But how? What's the word?
Faith and Will can move mountains, and horses, too.
Pooh! Here's the horse—what more do you need, Peer?
> *(donning paraphernalia)*

Sir Peter Gynt, a Turk, too, from head to toe!
Well, you never know what Fate has in store for you!
> *(mounting)*

Giddyap, Blackie! I mean, Whitie—let's go!
Saddled and bridled like the Grand Emir!
Great riders are known by their riding-gear!

SCENE VI

*The lone tent of an Arab chief on an oasis. Peer Gynt, in
Eastern garb, reclines on a cushioned divan, drinking coffee
and smoking a long Turkish pipe. Anitra and a bevy of girls
sing and dance before him.*

CHORUS OF GIRLS

Summon the Faithful!
Welcome the Prophet!
>   Allah commands!
>   Strike up the drums,
>   He comes, he comes,
>   To lead his bands,
>   Across the sands.

Call all the Faithful!
Bring out the lute
And the dulcet flute.
All hail the Prophet!
Allah commands!
Strike up the drums,
He comes, he comes,
Across the sands.

ANITRA

Swift is his milk-white steed,
Swift as the gazelle in speed.
Bow the head and bend the knee.
His eyeball flashes like a coal,
The Seraph in his soul.
Across the desert he came,
In pearls shining like a lamp,
In gold with the Master's stamp,
In the desert night.
Bow the head and bend the knee.
Where he rode there was light,
Behind him all was dark.
Through the Simoon's dreadful dance,
Across the void he came,
Like a mortal clothed.
Kaaba's now an empty name,
The Prophet has proclaimed!

CHORUS OF GIRLS

Bring out the lute,
And the dulcet flute,
Strike up the drums!
The Prophet comes!

PEER GYNT

'Tis said, No one's a prophet in his own country.
However, this is surely the life for me.
Hindsight shows many my holdings were shady,
To climb up the golden ladder to fame
Is like building on sand—you've a shaky frame.

Again, to bedizen yourself with gold and all that,
To bedeck yourself with the conventional plug-hat;
To make the rabble fawn and look up to you,
Is the height of folly, but mostly, I say, ego;
Yet sometimes they serve as touchstones to our friends,
But here the applause and comedy ends.
The Prophet is different—you know where you stand,
If one salutes you, it's for yourself—that's grand.
'Tis never for your worldly goods—you owe
Nothing to chance or accident. O no!
A Prophet, ah yes, 'tis a new life for me,
And I fell heir to the office unexpectedly.
I was ordained for this—The Chosen One!
And lo! the Prophet came—'twas only natural,
And I have no desire to deceive anyone.
Of course, there's some difference between lying
And Prophecy. I can always turn back—
I'm in no way bound—I'm not upon a rack—
I can go anytime—everything's confidential.
My horse stands ready—I can leave in a twinkling.

ANITRA
(approaching the tent door)

Prophet and master!—

PEER
What is it, my slave?

ANITRA

The sons of the desert stand without and crave
A glimpse and a word of the Prophet!

PEER

Tell them to wait with patience, but I regret
I must hear their prayer from a distance.
No man shall enter here under any circumstance.
Men, my child, are a barefaced, worthless crew,
Filthy, atrocious rascals, through and through.
Ah, Anitra, my sweet ward, you do not know
How oft they contrived to swindle me.
But come, children, sing and dance, let's be merry,
The Prophet would banish all care and sorrow.

THE GIRLS
(dancing)

The Prophet is good, but the Prophet is wary
Of the sins that the sons of the desert practice;
The Prophet is kind; all praise his charity;
He shall lead the penitent to his Paradise.

PEER
(His eyes follow Anitra during the dance)

Her legs are as nimble as a ballet model.
What a sweet little package—a dainty morsel.
Of course, some of her curves are a bit abnormal—
Not up to the standard norm for beauty.
But what is beauty? Just mere convention,
Only small change, presumptuous, effete;
Sometimes the extravagant seems more refined,
When one's fed up with the conventional kind.
Women and men, too, never run true to perfection—
They're too fat or too lean, too young or too old,
While the in-betweens are insipid and cold.
She'd look better if she washed her hands and feet,
You might even call it a qualification!
Anitra, come to my divan!

ANITRA
(approaching)
To hear is to obey!

PEER

You're bewitching, my child. The Prophet is touched.
I'll make you an Houri without delay.

ANITRA
Impossible, master!

PEER
This is no idle jest.
I'm in earnest, really. Be comforted!

ANITRA
But I have no soul!

PEER

Then you shall have one!

ANITRA

But how, master?

PEER

Leave that to me—you're so modest.
I see I'll have to take you in tow, my girl.
No soul? No brains? Of course, I had a suspicion.
But, pshaw! We'll have to find room for a soul.
O yes, I was right. There's room for a large soul.
I see. You'll never make a dent in this world.
But never mind, just relax, you'll get by somehow.

ANITRA

The Prophet is kind!

PEER

Speak up, don't be bashful!

ANITRA

I'd rather have—

PEER

Come out with it, woman!

ANITRA

I don't care so much about having a soul,
I'd rather have—

PEER

What?

ANITRA

(pointing to his turban)

That lovely opal!

PEER

(Enraptured, gives her the jewel.)

Anitra! Anitra! A true daughter of Eve!
You're charming, you attract me—for I am a man,
And as a famous poet once said, I believe,
"Das ewig Weibliche zieht uns an!"

SCENE VII

Moonlight. Palmgrove outside Anitra's tent. Peer Gynt, with
an Arabian lute in his hands, is sitting beneath a tree. His
beard and his hair are clipped, and he looks much younger.

PEER GYNT
(plays and sings)

I locked the door to Paradise
    And threw away the key.
Before the Northwind my ship flies,
While lovely women, fearful wise,
    Weep by the lonely sea.

Southward I sailed the bounding sea
    To many a strange land,
Where lordly palms sway proud and free.
I lost my ship unknowingly,
    Upon the golden strand.

A Ship of the Desert I bought
    And four good legs had he;
Forty roving nomads I fought,
And many, many more I sought,
    Over the broad sand-sea.

Look child, see this lovely ruby,
    Turquoise and amethyst,
With pale opal and sapphire blue,
And a lavaliere sweet as you—
    All for a lover's kiss.

So still? I wonder if she heard my song?
Disrobing behind the arras? Silent her tongue.
What's that? Sounds like a bull-frog serenade.
What more? Love sighs? Songs of some young blade?
No, that's snoring! Sleep my Arab beauty, sleep.
O sweet nightingale, cease thy plaintive tale.
You couldn't win a prize at a poultry show.
O well, sing on Philomela, sing soft and low,
A singer thou art like myself. Music's our art,

To comfort and enthrall every tender heart,
And to hear my darling, in her own way,
Is the pinnacle of passion's crowning bliss.
I ask not for wine—let me plant a kiss
On the cup. She's awake! Now begins the day!

ANITRA
(from the tent)

Did you call, master?

PEER

Yes, my love, it was I.
I was roused by a dozen cats nearby.

ANITRA

Cats could not disturb me, master.

PEER

What was it?

ANITRA

O, spare me!

PEER

What was it, daughter?

ANITRA

O, I blush, sire!

PEER
(coming closer)

You mean the emotions I was feeling
When I gave you the opal?

ANITRA
(horrified)
Disgusting!

Master, don't compare yourself to an old cat!

PEER

Tut, tut, my child, from the lover's view
Tom-cat and the Prophet see eye to eye.

ANITRA

Pooh, master! Your jokes are all to flat!

PEER

My little friend, no man can truthfully deny
A man's looks are deceiving. I'm full of jest too.
My office forces me to assume a solemn mask.
All this is superficial—I'd rather bask
With the elite. Avaunt Prophet, I'm just Peer!
From now I shall be myself, we'll forget the seer.

(Seats himself under a tree and draws Anitra close to him).

Come dear, feel the palm's cool fans
And the leaves' caressing breezes.
Come, lie beneath these lofty trees,
We'll dream of love and caravans—
I will whisper, you will laugh,
I will laugh, you will whisper.

ANITRA

(lying at his feet)

All your fine words are sweet as music—
I could understand it better in Arabic.
Tell me, All-seeing One, can your daughter
Get a soul by listening?

PEER

Mark your tutor.
In due time you'll be endowed with a soul.
When Allah, the All-Wise, writes in the sky "Der Tag!"
I'll begin your lessons, dust off the old school-bag.
But we'll not waste the balmy nights with rigmarole;
By no means! The teacher then becomes the lover!

ANITRA

Say on, O master, I see sparkling gems
When you speak, and a thousand diadems!

PEER

Extremes in wisdom is fully "preserved
In quotations;" cowardice is cruelly exalted;
Overworked truth is wisdom upside down,
When the brain-bound savant becomes a clown.
Many a blatant king has lost both head and crown.
Look, I could compress the world in my turban,

But that's silly! I'd be crazy as Ramman!
What is life, my child?

ANITRA

Teach me from the Koran.

PEER

Life means gliding safely down the River of Time.
Manhood comes only with age and season.
Old age ends in dotage, old crows moult their plumage.
Youth! youth! I mean to reign a Sultan in my prime!
Not on Gyntiana's shores, but enthroned anon
Upon the freshness of beauty, endless dreams.
I bestowed my love, child, on you for this reason.
You shall be my life's caliphate—mine alone.
I shall enthrall you with gold and priceless gems,
But should we part, then life is over—done—
At least for you. Now, on second thought it seems
Fortunate your head's void. With a soul one
May get some queer ideas. As a token, dear,
I fasten this bangle around your ankle—so.
I'll be your soul, by proxy—ah, status quo!

(Anitra snores)

Asleep! In one ear and out the other ear.
Pshaw! I still have the old power of lying!
It transports her softly to the land of dreams.

(Laying jewels in her lap)

Here are jewels! Here are more beseeming!
Sleep, my child! For this I have won a crown
Of Victory that Peer Gynt can call his own!

SCENE VIII

*A caravan route. The oasis is seen in the background. Peer
Gynt comes galloping across the desert on his white horse,
    holding Anitra in front of him on the saddle.*

ANITRA

Let me be or I'll bite!

PEER

You'll never regret—

ANITRA

What do you intend to do?

PEER

We'll play hawk and dove!
Carry you off! We'll frisk about a bit, my love!

ANITRA

For shame! And to think you an old Prophet!

PEER

O you taunt me for my age. I'm not old,
You little goose. Not at all—I'm a lover bold!

ANITRA

Let me go, please! I must go home, Prophet!

PEER

You make me laugh. What home, you little flirt?
We can't face your father—he scours the desert.
The Prophet must keep aloof of his tribe—
The less seen, the more veneration they subscribe;
I never tarry very long in one place—
Familiarity breeds contempt and you lose face,
And I find these sons of the desert a farce—
My popularity wanes, prayers are scarce.

ANITRA

But *are* you a Prophet?

PEER

I am your master!
(*Tries to kiss her*)
Tut, my sweet sweeting, I'm your true lover!

ANITRA

O give me that beautiful opal ring!

PEER

It's all yours, dear. I'll give you anything!

ANITRA

Your words are like mellifluous madrigals!

PEER

O such bliss, such love, no one can gainsay!
Let me down—like a slave, I'll lead your palfrey!
         (Hands her the whip—dismounts)
There you are, my little rosebud, my darling,
I'll wade through the desert sand, and sweat,
Maybe get a sunstroke, but don't fret,
I'm young and frolicsome—your Prince Charming.
Jokes and High-jinks are youth's stock-in-trade.
I may be old, but I feel like a young blade.
You'd understand if you were not so headstrong
And dumb. I'm full of vim—ever so young!

ANITRA

Yes, you are young, but have you more jewels?

PEER

I admit I'm young. Here are opals and beryls.
If only I had some feathers for my brow,
I'd show you how the Indians dance a pow-wow!

            (Dances and sings)

          I'm a strutting Chanticleer,
          Come ducky, lend me your ear.
             With a merry note,
             I'll atune my throat—
          A loud cock-a-loodle-loo,
          Cock-a-loodle I shall crow—
          Let the desert-sands echo!

ANITRA

Be careful, Prophet, I'm afraid you'll melt;
Let me have that bag that hangs from your belt!

PEER

O such tender concern! Here, take my purse!
Gold to loving hearts is ever a curse!

            (Sings and dances)

Love, when I look upon you,
My poor heart goes pit-a-pat.
I'm frisky as a tom-cat
On a cold Saturday night—
That's what mighty love can do,
My love, my heart's delight!

ANITRA

Prophet, poet and dancer, all in one!

PEER

O, forget the Prophet! Come, let's put on
Each other's clothes—

ANITRA

Your caftan is too long,
Your belt's too wide—I prefer a sarong!

PEER
(kneeling)

Inflict some vehement sorrow upon me;
Sweet is the pleasure that is born of pain;
Like a queen in my castle you shall reign!

ANITRA

To your Paradise—how far, O Worthy?

PEER

A thousand miles or so—

ANITRA

My poor swain!

PEER

You shall see
The soul I promised you, but look—

ANITRA

Pooh! I crave
No soul, Prophet! But you asked for pain!

PEER
(rising)

Aye, a short one that will last for a few days!

ANITRA

You asked for it, All-wise One—Anitra obeys!

(Raps him across the fingers with the whip; dashes away.)
Farewell!

PEER

(Stands for a long while, thunderstruck)
I'll be damned! She was a *sweet crook!*

SCENE IX

The same, an hour later. Peer Gynt, slowly and thoughtfully, discards his Turkish costume bit by bit. Lastly he takes his traveling cap out of his coat and puts it on.

PEER GYNT

(Throwing turban away)

There goes the Turk and Prophet—I'm Peer once more.
Those heathen customs I cannot endure.
I'm lucky that it's only a matter of clothes,
And not bred in the bone, as the old saw goes.
It behooves a man to live like a Christian,
To shun the gaudy peacock dress of a Pagan,
To fear God, walk in His steps, break no laws,
Be yourself and keep out of the devil's claws.
These folks will some day say kind words, revere
Your name, and place a wreath upon your bier.

(taking a few steps)

Why, that ornery rascal, that little faker!
She surely took me, hook, line and sinker.
She was on the verge of turning my head.
Well, that's over, thank heaven! The less said
The better. But it's some comfort, I was off guard
In a weak moment. Soothsaying's a hazard—

That's not my forte. After all, I'm still a man—
In courting the little goose, I was only human.
Ha! There's no fool like an old fool, they say.

(Bursts out laughing)

Sir Peter Gynt singing, dancing, so blithe and gay;
Strumming the lute, crowing like a rooster.
Ha! Then plucked by a hen of every feather.
Yes, plucked, plucked clean to the bone—
I have only a trifle I can call my own.

(feeling in his pockets)

A little cash in hand, in America some holdings—
Not quite broke, not enough to hobnob with kings.
I feel better foot-loose, with no trappings—
Horses, coachmen, servants and the like.
No! I'm not washed up yet. I'll soon strike
Something good; of course, as a merchantman
And lover, I'm finished. However, I don't plan
To retrace my steps. No, I'll turn over a new leaf.
I must find some noble task. I'll find relief—
Say in my autobiography. No, 'twould be too long,
I'll just write a history of the world—a song
Of humanity, with all its joy and grief.
Like a feather, I'll float down history's stream,
And make it live again, as in a dream.

(With quiet emotion)

See brave men battle for truth and right,
Of course, I'll keep safely out of sight;
See saints and sages sacrificed for spite;
See war, the trade of Kings, wax and wane;
See the conquering heroes come and go—
In short, I'll skim off the cream of history,
I'll give them something different and new,
I can always fall back on my lying.
Aye, I'll bury myself in antiquity
And forsake the beaten paths of the living.
The present's not worth a pair of shoe-strings.
Here, I think, I may find myself again.
Proud and vain are the ways of men and kings—

Their souls have no wings, their deeds no salt.
                    (Shrugs his shoulders)
And woman—ah, that's the Maker's fault!

SCENE X

*A summer day, far up North. A hut in the woods. A door,
with a large wooden bar, stands open. Above the door a
pair of large antlers. A small herd of goats grazes by the side
of the hut. Solveig, now middle-aged but fair and comely,
sits and spins outside in the sunlight.*

SOLVEIG
(Looks down the path and sings)
The seasons slowly come and go;
   I know you will return some day;
   Here I abide, lad, and spin and pray
As I promised, lad, long, long ago.
    (calls the goats, and spins and sings again)
God guard you, wherever you are;
   God bless you when you kneel in prayer;
   I'll abide in thee, lad, forever;
If above, lad, I'll meet you there.

SCENE XI

In Egypt. Dawn at the foot of the Statue of Memnon.

PEER GYNT
(Comes on, stops and looks around.)
Just the right place for Gynt, the Historian
To begin. For the present I'm an Egyptian,
And, of course, with the emphasis on I.
Next, I'll take ancient Assyria on high.
To begin right back at the world's creation

Would lead only to trouble and confusion.
Anyhow, Bible lore's not popular to-day—
I'll just take a bird's-eye view, as they say.
I'll abridge or elaborate here and there,
Pick out the high spots in true Gynt flair—
When you describe a horse you don't enumerate
All the hairs in his tail.

(Sits down on stone)

           Here I'll rest and wait,
Until Memnon sings his usual dawn-song,
Then I shall join the pyramid throng
After breakfast, and look inside, if I have
The time. Next, around the Red Sea by land,
Where I may discover King Potiphar's grave.
Next I'll turn Asiatic. In Babylon I'll stand
And gaze at the famous hanging gardens;
With a bound I'll land on Troy's wasting walls,
Hop across the Hellespont to famed Athens—
Carefully scan the ancient Greek book-stalls,
Perchance, some forgotten philosopher dig up;
See where Socrates drank the fatal cup,
Find out where Diogenes hung his lantern,
And, lastly, survey the heroic Leonidas Pass—
But, hold—they're at war—I'll keep out of the fracas.
Well, there's no hurry, I can always return.

(Looks at his watch)

It's a shame the time Sol takes to come up.
My time is precious—now, as I was saying—

(Rises and listens.)

Hark! I hear a strange murmuring—

(Sunrise)

MEMNON'S STATUE
(Sings)

From the ashes of the godling
Arise rejuvenating
Birds ever singing.

Zeus, the All-Knowing
Bred them to transmogrify.
O Owls of Wisdom,
Where sleep my birds? Come,
Solve the song's riddle or die!

PEER

So eerie!—I will swear I heard music
From the statue, now rising, now falling,
Music of past ages—reverberating.
I'll make a note for some future critic.

(Makes notation)

"The Statue sang quite audibly,
The words I couldn't make out clearly.
The whole thing's a hallucination—
Otherwise, nothing worthwhile to mention."

SCENE XII

The Great Sphinx near the village of Gizeh. The spires and minarets of Cairo in the background. Peer Gynt examines the Sphinx carefully, now through his eyeglasses, now through his hollowed hands.

PEER GYNT

That homely face looks very familiar.
I really can't place him now, but somewhere
In my travels we've met. Memnon reminds me
Of the Troll King—so cold and unmovable,
With only a stone-slab for his eerie throne.
But this monster, half human, half lion—
Does he come to me from some fairy story,
Or from experience, or a real person?
Ha! It's old Boyg, whom I hit with a cudgel—
That is, I dreamt I did, as I lay in a fever.

(Going closer.)

The eyes are the same, the mouth as wide as ever,
Not quite so large, yet a little more cunning,

But in the main points they are just like twins.
Hi there Boyg! Now you dress in lion skins.
Do you remember the night I banged your shins?
Still snoop around, Boyg? Still good at riddling?
Let's try and see, or do you still remember?
Hi, Boyg!

(Calls out)
Who are you?

A VOICE

(Behind the Sphinx)

Ach, Sphinx, wer bist du?

PEER

What! Echo answers in German! Incredible!

VOICE

Wer bist du?

PEER

Ah, it speaks quite fluently.
My observation is new. Just a note in the margin.
(Writes)
"Echo in German; accent distinctly Berlin."

(Begriffenfeldt comes from behind the Sphinx)
BEGRIFFENFELDT

A man!

PEER

O you were the ventriloquist!
"The mystery is clearing up." *(Writes)*

BEGRIFFENFELDT

(cutting up)
Pardon me, I can't resist
Asking, What brings you to this place, mein Herr?

PEER

A belated visit to an old friend of mine.

BEGRIFFENFELDT

The Sphinx?

PEER
(nods)
Yes, I've known him for a long time.

BEGRIFFENFELDT
Splendid! and I have had a hectic night—
The way my temples throb, it is a fright.
Do you know him? Speak, man! What is he?

PEER
O, that's very simple. He is Himself, mein Herr!

BEGRIFFENFELDT
(with a bound)
Ha! Like a flash I see the solution
To 'Life's riddle. True, true, he is himself!

PEER
Yes, indeed, he says so without reservation.

BEGRIFFENFELDT
Himself! The day of awakening is here!
(Takes off his hat.)
Your name, kind sir?

PEER
I am Peer Gynt, mein Herr.

BEGRIFFENFELDT
(jubilantly)
Peer Gynt! The Unknown! Behold!
Peer Gynt! I mean—The Great Unknown!
The Messiah, whose coming was foretold!

PEER
Then you came here to meet—

BEGRIFFENFELDT
Peer Gynt! Profound! Enigmatic! Wise!
Unrivalled in thought—every word a prize!
What are you?

PEER
(modestly)
I ever try to be of good report,
To be Myself—for the rest, here's my passport.

BEGRIFFENFELDT
(scanning passport)
Enigmatic, too—from top to the very bottom!
(Seizing him by the hand)
I have found the Kaiser! Come to my bosom!

PEER

Kaiser?

BEGRIFFENFELDT
Come—to Cairo!
PEER
I'm really—
BEGRIFFENFELDT
(dragging Peer along)
The Interpreters' Kaiser—no one but Himself!

SCENE XIII

*Cairo. A large courtyard with high walls surrounded by
buildings. Barred windows. Iron Cages. Three guards in the
court, a fourth enters.*

THE NEWCOMER
Schafmann, where has the Herr Director gone?

A GUARD
He left early this morning—before dawn.

FIRST GUARD
Something has been worrying him of late
For last night—

ANOTHER
Hush, he's unlocking the gate!

(Begriffenfeldt leads Peer in, locks the gate, pockets key.)

PEER
(aside)
He seems to be a remarkably gifted man;
At times he's almost beyond comprehension.
(Looking around)
So this is your guild? I thought such—

BEGRIFFENFELDT
Here they are, my seventy scholars, every man
An Interpreter—a King in his own dominion,
Of late grown to one hundred and sixty.
(Calling to guards)
Mikkal, Schlingelberg, Schafmann, Deutsch,
Every one of you! Quick into your hutch!

THE GUARDS
What! We?

BEGRIFFENFELDT
Yes, the world's gone topsy-turvy!
We must get in line!
(Forces them in cage.)
This morning the Great Peer
Came to us. The rest you can guess.
(Locks the cage and throws the key into a well.)

PEER
Herr Doctor and Director, I profess—

BEGRIFFENFELDT
I am neither one nor the other now.
Can you keep a secret, mein Herr?
You must know—

PEER
(uneasy)
What is it?

BEGRIFFENFELDT
Don't get excited!

PEER
I shall try.

BEGRIFFENFELDT
(Takes him aside and whispers.)
Absolute Reason expired last night at eleven!

PEER
God help me, mein Herr! You mortify—

BEGRIFFENFELDT
It's deplorable, unpleasant—I'll be outspoken.
Up till to-day the place was an asylum!

PEER
A madhouse?

BEGRIFFENFELDT
Ha! You see!

PEER
(aside)
I'll make a memorandum—
The man's like a lot of people in this world,
Crazy, but doesn't know it! *(Moving away)*
(Aloud)   Expired, you say?

BEGRIFFENFELDT
(follows)
I hope you follow me. He's really not dead,
He's beside himself—turned inside out instead,
Like Münchausen's fox, you know the story.

PEER
(moving away)
Excuse me, sir.

BEGRIFFENFELDT
(confronting him)
No, no, it was an eel! I hurled
A nail through his eye, a stick round his head,
A slit, a jerk, and out he popped!—

PEER

Crazy!

BEGRIFFENFELDT

Now this exodus is clear as daylight,
This Self-Exit from our spatial and temporal
Shell is self-adjusting. Eventually
Conforming with Reason's newest proposal;
As in my case, at eleven o'clock last night
The so-called Abnormal became sane,
And, as we shall see, the Normal insane!

PEER

It's time for me to go—

BEGRIFFENFELDT

That's a good hint.
(Opens a door, calls out)
Come out, Reason is dead. The hour has come!
A new era's proclaimed! Long live Peer Gynt!

PEER

But, my dear sir—

BEGRIFFENFELDT

Come, hail the dawn of freedom!
Meet your new Kaiser!
(The inmates come out slowly, one by one, into the court.)

PEER

Kaiser?

BEGRIFFENFELDT

We welcome—

PEER

I'm flattered by the great honor, you see—

BEGRIFFENFELDT

Tut, tut, now forget your false modesty.

PEER

At least give me some time—you strike me dumb!

BEGRIFFENFELDT

What? The man who fathomed the Sphinx's riddle,
A man who is Himself—

PEER

True, yet I feel jumpy.
I am myself in every way. The trouble
I think here, every man is Outside Himself!

BEGRIFFENFELDT

O no, you are entirely mistaken.
Every man here is without bounds, his own warden,
Even to the utmost consequences.
Every man shuts himself in a cask of Self,
Each cask stopped up with a bung of Self,
And seasoned in the same well of Self.
Every man bears his own griefs and woes,
Every man thinks and does as he pleases,
And in due form we'll our Kaiser christen.
That, Kaiser, is the way our little world goes!

PEER

O, would the devil—

BEGRIFFENFELDT

Come, don't be downcast.
Every strange thing eventually becomes unmasked.
"Oneself."—Here's a specimen you shall see.
I will choose one of our guests at random.
                    (To a gloomy figure)
Good day, Hu-hu. How goes the word conundrum?
Do you think you'll ever solve the mystery?

HU-HU

Generation after generation, doctor, dies,
Bogged down with their own silly fallacies.
                    (To Peer)
You're a candidate, sir—will you listen?

PEER
(bowing)

By all means—

HU-HU

Lend me your ear, then.
Far away in an eastern land,
Lies the Malabarian strand.

Hollander and Portuguese
Now rule and live the life of ease,
Albeit our own aborigines
Have confused our native speech.
In primordial times there ruled
The Orang-outang—unfettered,
Swung and hopped from tree to tree,
Shrieking and yodeling in his glee.
Foreigners have now upset his liberty,
And polluted our forest-tongue.
Ah, centuries have come and gone,
Mute is the forest primeval,
No growl or shriek is heard withal.
Listen! From the wuthering wolds,
From the crimson colored clouds,
Come naught but words, words, words,
Bat-like voices, and discords.
This is unfair to everybody.
For years I have sought to restore
Our long-lost native forest-speech,
Uphold our sacred right to howl.
I, too, screech in my poetry,
And teach my poor people to screech
In their folk-songs, but it is plain
All my labors have been in vain.
I thank you for this courtesy,
And now, sir, I crave your counsel.

PEER
(aside)

It is said, my friend, 'tis best be howling
With the wolves than ever groveling.
(aloud)
My friend, I distinctly recollect
There's trees in Morocco whose retrospect
I'll never forget. Here Orang-outangs
Have neither songs nor teachers—only whangs
And bangs, and their speech sounded Malabar—
Why don't you go home? You're a great scholar.
Get a tail, professor, and teach them grammar.

HU-HU

Thank you, sir, for lending me your ear.
I shall do as you say, my Kaiser!
(with a gesture)
East, thou hast disowned thy singer!
West, thou hast gained a new leader!

BEGRIFFENFELDT

He's all wound up in himself, I would say—
Self-contained, self-centered in every way.
Now, this next one's completely restored.
Changed last night on the dot with the word.
How goes it to-day, King Apis, mighty lord?
(to a Fellah with a mummy on his back)

THE FELLAH
(wildly to Peer)

Am I King Apis?

PEER
(getting behind the doctor)
I'm not quite at home here,
But, judging from your tone, sir, you appear—

THE FELLAH

You're lying!

BEGRIFFENFELDT

Go on, your Highness, start anywhere.

THE FELLAH
(to Peer)

Do you see this thing on my back?
   King Apis was his name.
But now he's called a mummy.
   Alas, such is fame!

He built the mighty Pyramids,
   He created the great Sphinx,
And right and left he fought the Turks,
   So the professor thinks.

Now all of Egypt worshipped
   The sacred Bull of Memphis

In every temple in the land,
    Dear as a tear of Isis.

Now, I'm this very King Apis,
    And that is clear as day.
Just in case you don't understand,
    I'll explain it this way.—

Once upon the chase King Apis
    Alighted from his steed,
And blest a portion of the field
    For my father to seed.

The field which King Apis manured
    Nourished me with its corn,
And if you still demand more proof,
    I have here the King's horn.

I call it downright injustice,
    No one admits I'm right,
For by birth I am King Apis,
    But a Fellah bedight.

Now, can't you give me some advice.
    Can I perpetuate
My good name and become famous,
    Like King Apis, The Great?

PEER

Build bigger pyramids, Junior,
    Hew out a greater Sphinx,
And fight like your ancestor,
    And drive out all Turks.

THE FELLAH

Indeed, a plausible story.
    A fellah—hungry lice,
I can scarce keep my little cell
    Free from the rats and mice.

Sir, you must something else devise
    That'll save me from the rack,

And make me great like King Apis
I carry on my back.

PEER

Why not hang yourself, your Highness,
And end this earthly mess,
Rest in peace in some quiet grave—
That's the advice I have.

THE FELLAH

I'll do it, sir! Give me a rope!
To the gallows, boys!
Farewell, O fickle, fawning Hope,
And visionary joys!

(Exits—Prepares to hang himself)

BEGRIFFENFELDT

Now, that's what I call a personality.
There is madness in his very method!

PEER

He's going to hang himself! Help us, God,
I cannot control my thoughts! I feel ill!

BEGRIFFENFELDT

Calm yourself, sir. It's only transitory!

PEER

That's what you think! I must leave now, I will—

BEGRIFFENFELDT
(holding him)

Are you crazy?

PEER

No, not yet! God forbid!

(An uproar. The Minister Hussein rushes forth.)

HUSSEIN

I hear our Kaiser is here—that's splendid!
(to Peer)
Is that you?

PEER
(in desperation)
Yes, I am your Kaiser!

HUSSEIN
There's some correspondence to be answered!

PEER
(tearing his hair)
Yes, yes, go on! the madder the better!

HUSSEIN
Will you do me the courtesy of taking a dip?
(bowing deeply)
I am a Pen!

PEER
(bowing more deeply)
Let's see your penmanship,
I am a very rare piece of paper!

HUSSEIN
Listen to my story—I'll be outspoken,
They take me for a sand-cellar, but I'm a pen!

PEER
And mine's hardly worth mentioning, Sir Pen,
I'm a blank sheet that's never been penned!

HUSSEIN
What I'm good for, no one can understand,
Except they only use me for blotting-sand!

PEER
Pshaw! Once I was a Princess's bookmark,
And like a Thespian ghost, I haunted Plutarch!

HUSSEIN
Just think, Kaiser, what a distasteful life—
A Pen that never felt the edge of a knife!

PEER
(with a leap)
Ho! Fancy a reindeer leaping through the sky,
And plunging into a tarn without a cry!

HUSSEIN

O knife, I'm dull. Come sharpen me! I've heard
The Pen is more mighty than the Sword!

PEER

O, a thousand pities for the world, Lord,
That has forsaken Him, and lost His word!

BEGRIFFENFELDT

Here's a knife!

HUSSEIN
(seizing it)
This is all balderdash!
What a pleasure to cut!
(Cuts his throat)

BEGRIFFENFELDT
(stepping aside)
O, you must not splash!

PEER
(terrified)

Hold him!

HUSSEIN
Hold, yes, that's the correct word!
Hold! hold my pen for me! Let me record—
Postscript: Little I care what the world will think,
Say I am worn out, and writ in sanguine ink!

PEER
(dizzy)

What shall I do? What am I? Great, greater!
I'm all that thou wilt, a Turk, a sinner,
A hill-troll! Come, help me before I faint!
I can't just now think of my Patron Saint—
But come, anyway—the madmen's protector!
(faints)

BEGRIFFENFELDT
(With a straw wreath in his hand, leaps astride Peer.)
Ha! In the mire he's enthroned,

Beside Himself! Let him be crowned!

> *(Places wreath on Peer's head and shouts)*

Long live Selfdom's Kaiser!

                    SCHAFMANN
                  (from his cell)

Es lebe hoch der grosse Peer!

ACT V

SCENE I

*On ship on the North Sea off the Norwegian Coast. Sunset.
A storm is brewing.*

*Peer Gynt, now a vigorous old man with snow-white hair and
beard, stands aft on the poop. His clothes are somewhat
worse for wear, sailor-like, with a pea jacket and high boots.
He looks weatherbeaten and has a somewhat harder expres-
sion. The Captain is beside the Pilot. The Crew is forward.*

PEER GYNT
(Leans with his arms on the railing and gazes toward the land.)
Look at Hallingskarv in his winter clothes,
Swaggering above in the evening glow;
Behind him, Brother Jokel at his elbow,
Basking in the soft flickering shadows;
In the background lies Folgefänn so bright,
Like a maiden dressed in spotless white.
How inspiring! Even a niveous granite shaft
Proclaims His might and shows His handicraft!

THE CAPTAIN
(shouting forward)
Two men to the wheel! Hoist a light!

PEER
A stiff breeze—

CAPTAIN
We'll have a storm before night.

PEER
Can one see the Rondë Hills from the sea?
142

CAPTAIN

No, they lie way back behind the snow fields.

PEER

Or Blähö?

CAPTAIN

No, but the rigging yields
A good view of Galdhöpiggen in clear weather.

PEER

And Harteig?

CAPTAIN
(pointing)

I'd say about over there.

PEER

I thought so.

CAPTAIN

You seem to be at home here.

PEER

When I sailed from home I passed by here.
The dregs, they say, hang on till the very last.
(Spits and gazes at the coast.)

Over there where the blue screes are masked,
Where the valleys like ravines appear,
Skirting the fjords like a sparkling strand,
(looking at the captain)
Lives the backbone of Norway—my homeland!
Not many homes?

CAPTAIN

Aye, few and far between.

PEER

Shall we dock in the morning?

CAPTAIN

Yes, I imagine.

PEER

It grows thick in the west.

CAPTAIN

Yes, so it does.

PEER

By the way, when I settle my account I've a mind
To do a turn for the crew, as the word goes.

CAPTAIN

I thank you.

PEER

Only a small token, let's say,
I grubbed for gold and lost all in my day.
What I've salvaged is in the cabin's till—
All I've left—the rest's gone to the devil!

CAPTAIN

Aye, enough to make a good showing at home.

PEER

I have neither relatives nor heirs to comb
The pier for a rich old curmudgeon.

CAPTAIN

Here's the storm—

PEER

Should your crew need any cash, call upon
Peer Gynt. I can help them, within reason.

CAPTAIN

That's kind. You'll find most of them poor;
They've all got wives and children to be sure.
With their wages they can hardly make ends meet,
So, whoever adds to their treasure a mite
Always makes their day of homecoming complete.

PEER

All married? Wives and children, you say?

CAPTAIN

Every man of them! But the cook, by the way,
Famine stalks in his home, night and day.

PEER

Wives and children await their homecoming?
I presume a day of joy and thanksgiving?

CAPTAIN

Yes, in their own way.

PEER

Suppose they return in the evening?

CAPTAIN

O, his wife will fix a treat, maybe a feast
For supper, and a bumper of brandy at least.

PEER

And then they snuggle like a bug in a rug,
While the sailor-father, with many a shrug,
Relates his latest voyage, and they ask him
A thousand questions, as if he were a pilgrim.

CAPTAIN

My men will appreciate your little present—

PEER

(banging his fist on the railing.)

I'll be damned if I do—not a cent!
Why should I fork out gold for other's brats,
I've worked too hard for my money! Rats!
There's no one waiting for old Peter Gynt!

CAPTAIN

O, do as you please—it's your money, Mr. Gynt!

PEER

That's right! Mine it is—that's no poppycock!
We'll settle accounts as soon as we dock.
My fare from Panama and a snifter of rum
For the men, but not a penny nor a crumb
For your crew, Captain! Blow me down, if I do!

CAPTAIN

I'll give you an accounting—every sou!
But, excuse me, a gale's brewing on the prow!
(He goes forward. It has become dark, lights are lit in the

cabin, the sea grows rougher. Fog and clouds gather.)

PEER

Think of it! A wife and a flock of children
At home to look forward to—what a delight
To have loved ones follow your voyage, then
A feast, a light, two lights. To me it is night.
Ha! I'll get the whole damned crew dead drunk.
There won't be a sober sailor on this junk,
And when they get home, there'll be hell to pay.
They'll scare their old spouse and the children
Out of their wits! The world, you know, goes by fits!

(Ship gives a lurch. Peer falls on the bulwark.)

Ah, that was a grand slam. It seems the sea
Is working overtime tonight, but up North here
The sea is bullheaded as ever, and angry—
Hark! Is that a scream?

THE WATCH
A wreck on the lee!

CAPTAIN
(amidship)

Hold starboard! Keep her close to the wind!

THE PILOT

How many men?

THE WATCH
I can only see three!

PEER

Lower the jolly, quick!

CAPTAIN
She'll flounder in the sea!
(goes forward)

PEER

There's no time to lose! *(to some of the crew)*
                    If you're men, you'll save them!
All you need is brains, courage and stratagem!

THE BOATSWAIN

It's impossible, sir!

PEER

They call again on the lee!
Here, cook! Show your mettle! Ten pound sterling!

THE COOK

Not me—not for twenty pounds in this snarling—

PEER

You dogs, you cowards, you chicken-hearted salts!
These men, too, have wives and children waiting!

BOATSWAIN

Patience is always sound!

CAPTAIN

We're close to the rocks!

PILOT

Their ship's gone down!

PEER

And all is silent! What a night!

BOATSWAIN

And three new widows were made in our sight!

(The storm increases and Peer goes aft.)

PEER

This shows that man has lost his faith and love,
And has lost, too, the respect of Him above.
God shows His might in divers ways, I grant—
More dangerous than playing with an elephant.
Still, this crew has openly flaunted His pleasure.
I'm guiltless—I offered my purse, my treasure.
I stand before Him with a conscience clear and pure.
Of course, it might be less on land than at sea;
At sea one must always follow the rabble,
Else you're just another ham in the smokehouse.
Pilots are a dime a dozen on calm billows,
But in danger they're sound asleep on their pillows!

In the past I've always been too chickenhearted,
And I get no thanks for the way I've been treated.
If I were younger, I'd shift my saddle,
See how it felt to be lord for awhile.
It's not too late! I'll have it noised about
Lundë, Peer's come home rich, then I'll set out
To buy back the old homestead, build a palace,
No one shall ever set foot in the place!
Aye, I'll put a sign on the door: No admittance!
Maybe a few friends by invitation.
I'll make them beg and cringe and whine at the gate.
Nary a penny will they get. Let Fate
Crack down on someone else for awhile,
It'll do me good to smile from my smug bastile!

THE STRANGE PASSENGER

(Emerging from the hatchway's gloom, he bows to Peer Gynt.)
How d'ye do!

PEER

Good evening! What! Who are you?

THE STRANGER

A fellow traveler!

PEER

I thought I was the only one!

THE STRANGER

A slight error, sir, which is now set aright!

PEER

Strange—I haven't seen you before tonight.

THE STRANGER

That is true—I only come out at night!

PEER

Are you ill? You are as pale as a ghost!

THE STRANGER

O no! Of my health I like to boast!

PEER

What a terrible storm!

THE STRANGER

Yes, a blessed one, sir.

PEER

A blessed one?

THE STRANGER

A blessed storm—it's bound to occur—
I can taste the salt water in my mouth. I can see
Wrecks and corpses floating on the sea!

PEER

God save us!

THE STRANGER

Ever see a man hung or drowned?

PEER

You're really uncanny!

THE STRANGER

All corpses grin when hung!
How they twist and turn and bite their tongue!

PEER

Enough, man!

THE STRANGER

Only one more question, I pray,
Should we strike a rock tonight in our way
And sink in the dark—

PEER

Do you think there's danger?

THE STRANGER

Yes, it's all recorded in the Book of the Dead!
But suppose I float and you drown instead?

PEER

Poppycock!

THE STRANGER

This is all plausible.

Of course, with one foot in the grave, we grow
Softhearted and charitable when we're through!

PEER

Money? So—(reaching for his pocket)

THE STRANGER
No! No! Just *will* me your body!

PEER

This is too much!

THE STRANGER
Ah, just your corpse, no more!
I need one more cadaver for my research work!

PEER

Get out!

THE STRANGER
But see what you can do for humanity!
I seek to discover the source of dreams; furthermore
To ascertain why you look and act like a Turk!

PEER

Get out!

THE STRANGER
Only a water-soaked body!

PEER

Blasphemer! Have you fathered these foamy blasts?
Will you shred our sails, uproot our masts,
Unman the decks, aye man, to sleep with the wrecks!

THE STRANGER
Yet one word more. I will meet you later.
Time and circumstance may change your mind!
(Bows politely)
We'll meet again when you're sinking, and resigned
To your fate, and in a much better humor!
(Goes towards cabin.)

PEER

An unsavory fellow, a scientific fakir
Of the first water.
                    (To passing boatswain)
        Who was that fellow?

BOATSWAIN

I didn't see a soul, sir!

PEER

                Rot! I'll look below!
                (To cabin boy)
Boy, who went down these steps just now?

THE BOY

                            The ship's dog, sir!

THE WATCH

Land close ahead!

PEER

        Where's my strong box and my trunk?
Bring them on deck!

BOATSWAIN

        More important work just now!

PEER

            (to captain)
Pardon me, I'll help the cook. I was only joking!

CAPTAIN

The jib's down!

A SAILOR

        And the foresail—we're sunk!

BOATSWAIN

        (shouting from forward)
Breakers under the bow!

CAPTAIN

        The ship's cracking!

(Ship strikes. Confusion.)

SCENE II

Off shore among the rocks and breakers. The ship sinks. The jolly containing two men is seen through the mist. A towering wave fills and capsizes the boat. A shriek is heard, and then all is still. Gradually the jolly reappears, upside down. Peer Gynt is seen clinging to the side of the boat.

PEER GYNT

Help! Help! A boat! Help, I'll be the next!
Save me, Good Lord—how goes the text?

THE COOK
(Coming up on the other side)

O God, my children! Give me a hand!
Have mercy, Father! Lead me to land!

PEER

Let go!

THE COOK

Let go!

PEER

I'll strike!

THE COOK

I'll strike, too!

PEER

Let go! The boat won't float us two!

THE COOK

I know it! Yield!

PEER

Give in!

THE COOK

Not on my life!

(In the fight one of the Cook's hands is hurt, but he clings on with the other.)

PEER

Take off your hand!

THE COOK

O, think of my babes and wife!

PEER

My life is just as sweet to me as yours is to you!
You had a chance to save a soul tonight, too!

THE COOK

You've had your life! I am still quite young!

PEER

Make up your mind before we both plunge—

THE COOK

Have mercy! Don't you believe in Christ?
You're an old man! You'll never be missed!
            (Screams and slips)
I'm drowning!

PEER
(seizing him)
            No, I have you by the hair!
Come, be a brave fellow, say the Lord's Prayer!

THE COOK

I don't remember—I'm thinking of the shore!

PEER

Come, I will start it off for you—"Our Father"—

THE COOK

"Give us this day"—

PEER
            Skip that part of the score!
Now you can spend your days below, sailor!

THE COOK
(Sinking)
"Give us this day our—"
            (Drowns)

PEER

He was himself to the end!

(Crawls on boat)

Where there is life there is always hope, my friend!

(The Strange Passenger catches hold of the boat)

THE STRANGER

Good morning, sir!—

PEER

What the—

THE STRANGER

I heard your cries.

I am glad, indeed, to find you alive.

I've never failed yet in my prophecies!

PEER

Let go! Let go! There's hardly room enough for one!

THE STRANGER

Just let me hold on! By treading the water I'll strive

Not to upset you! I'm sure I'll not drown!

By the way, Peer, what about your body?

PEER

Quiet!

THE STRANGER

The whole crew's lost!

PEER

Shut up!

THE STRANGER

Willingly. *(Silence)*

PEER

Well!

THE STRANGER

I'm silent!

PEER

What now, more deviltry?

THE STRANGER

I'm waiting!

PEER
(tearing his hair)
I'll go mad! Who are you?

THE STRANGER
(nodding)
Just friendly!

PEER

What are you up to?

THE STRANGER
What! Can't you place me?

PEER

The Devil!

THE STRANGER
(softly)
Does he light the paths of darkness
When we are beset with fear and distress?

PEER
And all the time I thought you were a parasite—
But now you seem to be a messenger of light!

THE STRANGER
Friend, did you ever experience in your life
Deep mental agony that cuts you like a knife?

PEER
I fear no man, sir, when I humbly walk
With God! Your words are only double talk!

THE STRANGER
My friend, did you ever once win the crown
From Fear, when it came to a real show down?

PEER
(looking at him)
So you think you've got me behind the eight-ball?
You'll find me a good shot—come one, come all!

THE STRANGER

Would your triumph be greater at home by the fire?

PEER

Pooh! Pooh, man! Your verse lacks poetic fire!

THE STRANGER

Where I come from they consider pathos
Just as important as the actor's bathos!

PEER

Everything has its place—what'll please the Pope
May taste to the Bishop like soft soap!

THE STRANGER

Those souls whose ashes rest in funeral urns
Will miss the buskined clown's quips and turns!

PEER

Be gone, old scarecrow! Now, let go your hand!
I shall not die! Not Peer! I shall reach land!

THE STRANGER

Cheer up! Don't be afraid! Why, man alive,
No one ever dies in the middle of Act Five!

PEER

Pooh! A moralist! Doesn't that beat the band!

SCENE III

*The last verse of a hymn is being sung at a funeral service in
a mountain churchyard. Peer Gynt, going by, stops at the gate.*

PEER GYNT

Poor soul, he goes the way of all flesh—dust to dust,
Thank heavens, it's not me. God is severe, but just!

THE VICAR
(at the grave)

Now that his poor soul has gone to meet His Lord,
Once a mere seedling, but now an empty pod,

Let us, dear friends, trace briefly in a word,
How this poor seedling grew in the sight of God,
And tread the paths his bruised feet have trod.

He was not wealthy, neither was he poor;
A pure, simple and humble man, without culture;
In bearing unmanly; in speech, all dross,
And to the last signed his name with a cross.
Like a hermit he was sad, lonely, and what's worse,
They say, he was scarce master in his own house.
Yet, every Sunday, he sidled furtively to his pew,
And found comfort and favor in His word like you.

He came, you know, from over Gudbrandsdale
As a lad, and settled down here in our vale,
Working here and there, an itinerant farmhand,
And you may recall, how, up to the very last,
He kept one hand hidden as if embarrassed,
And with the utmost diffidence seemed resigned—
The which stamped the lad in everyone's mind.
Year after year he kept aloof and seldom stirred
From home, and sphinx-like, rarely spoke a word,
And you no doubt, from time to time, had heard
He had only four fingers on his right hand.

'Twas long, long ago—I'll never forget:
War clouds were hovering over our land;
The whole town seemed on edge—I can see them yet.
I had sauntered up to the Lundë recruiting
Station on that memorial Monday morning—
At a long table sat a grizzled captain between
His aides, while the lads took their turn on the green,
Or loitered by the door; meanwhile, their singing
Flooded the room, and gave color to the scene.

For several hours, I saw the boys come and go,
Then came a lad, his face as white as snow.
His right hand was bandaged, and the poor youngster
Fought for words—his Adam's apple bobbled
Up and down like a bob on a fishing rod.
He bit his lip—flustered, abashed, he stammered,

In a muffled voice: "It may seem rather odd,
A scythe slipped, and cut off my index finger."

You could hear a pin drop, it was so still;
No one said a word—they gasped and stared
With open eyes, but no man was uncivil,
Yet he felt their scorn with a bowed head.
Now, the hoary captain arose, and was wroth,
Spat on the floor, and then with an oath,
Thundered "Begone," and pointed to the door.
The crowd parted, and fell back out of his way.
Shamefaced, the lad walked the plank that day,
Then, stumbling past the men, fled across the moor,
Through the woods, and up yon hillside he rolled.

A half year later he leased some land near Lomb,
Where the waste skirts the weeping hills, and built a home,
And cleared the land, and brought his betrothed, and child,
And mother. Later he married. Next year in the wild
Bottom land, fields of waving yellow corn tossed
Their golden heads, and he thrived in the sight of men.
Though in church he kept that right hand hidden,
At home those nine fingers did the work of ten.
And it came to pass one spring when the Northwind blew,
The rain fell, the streams rose, and the melting snow
Descended, and the flood came, and all was lost.

Their lives, however, were spared, thank God,
And with the patience of Job, he borrowed a horse,
And cleared the land, and builded a new house—
A better one this time he reared on higher ground.
Then came an avalanche, and swept all away,
And ere the smoke of the ruins had run its course,
He dug and dragged, plowed and planted the sod,
And long before the next winter came around,
He had, for the third time, builded his humble chalet.

He had three lads, three bright and well-favored lads;
They must go to school, but school was far from home,
And by devious ways they must clamber to Lomb;
Moreover, the paths and passes were dangerous

In winter. What did he do? This courageous
Peasant carried his little boys, one in each arm,
While the oldest lad clutched his father's cable-tow,
And trudged behind the best he could in the snow,
And in the same way they came back to the farm.

The boys grew up, and are now very rich men
Across the sea, but he, who slaved and toiled
To take them to school, was soon forgotten,
And he lived alone to the end on the old homestead.

He could see no farther than his own hand,
And those things that other men dearly cherished,
To him were utterly meaningless as the tinkling
Of cymbals—everything, his friends, his fatherland,
And all that was worth while in life, he missed.

But, all in all, he was a very humble man,
And a marked man from the day he scurried,
Crestfallen, from the draft-room, his right hand maimed
And swaddled. But do not condemn the man—
There is one thing that outshines his infamy
More than the glittering peak of yon Glittertinde.

Though God-fearing, he was no patriot; in the uplands
He toiled, and slaved, and struggled, early and late;
There he was himself, there in the hills he was great,
In his own little flock among the farmhands.
His life was like a song without the words—
A leaden lute whose heart-strings are silent, mute.
        Peace be with you, poor, silent warrior,
        We have lost a good friend and neighbor.

It's not for us to search the heart and the reins—
That's no task for the quick—no, let Him say the word!
And I pray that this man, who suffered the pains
Of Job, is no cripple in the eyes of the Lord.

(The little congregation breaks up—Peer comes forward.)

PEER

Now, that's what I call true Christianity!
I could not preach a better sermon myself.
The Vicar had no axe to grind, furthermore,
'Twas free from all ecclesiastical rancor,
And the gist of it was—Always Be Yourself!
And I dare say the sermon was very edifying.

Who was he? *(Looking down into the grave)*
                    Surely, he's not the poor stripling
Who chopped his hand the day I was hewing
Timber in the woods. Now, if I wasn't standing
Here all the time, I'd swear it was Myself,
Listening to the words of praise I deserve!
Yes, I can truly say with a little verve,
The Church, after all, is the true comforter—
We must be Ourselves, according to the psalter:
        Even as you sow, so shall you reap,
        Revere God and His commandments keep.

Now back home. Though narrow and steep my way,
Though Fate may be fickle and uninviting,
Still Old Peter Gynt shall go his *own* way,
And remain, alas—a poor, pious Viking!

SCENE IV

*A ramshackle shed stands on the bank of a dried up mill-
stream at the foot of the hillside. The ground is torn up and
the whole place is in waste. Up the hill stands an old farm-
house where there is a large gathering—some drinking, some
boisterous, at an auction in front of the house. Peer Gynt is
sitting on a wood-pile near the old millshed.*

PEER GYNT

Backwards or forwards, it is just as far,
In or out, up or down, I get nowhere.
Father Time slowly steals our years away
By pushing one day ahead of another;
Go roundabout, the Boyg used to say.

A MAN IN MOURNING

Now, there's nothing left but odds and ends.
(Sees Peer)
Strangers, too. God bless you! Waiting for friends?

PEER

Well met! A merry crowd—very inspiring;
Is it a christening or a wedding?

MAN IN MOURNING

No, it's a housewarming for the kindred,
And the bride is laid in a wormy bed.

PEER

Ah, yes, for the remnants the worms scramble—

MAN IN MOURNING

There the ditty ends, the rest is piffle—

PEER

Most ditties, dear sir, are mostly blather,
Old chestnuts, I remember as a youngster!

A LAD
(With a casting ladle)
Look! This once belonged to young Peer Gynt,
He used to stamp buttons like in a mint!

ANOTHER LAD

They say this was John Gynt's old money-sack!

A THIRD

A penny for this worn-out pedlar's pack!

PEER

Peer Gynt? Who was he?

MAN IN MOURNING
A sort of myth,
A kin to Death and the village blacksmith!

A MAN IN GREY

O you forget me, man—you must be mad!

MAN IN MOURNING

Aye, but don't forget the loft door at Hegstad!

MAN IN GREY
True, but you were never over dainty!

MAN IN MOURNING
If she does not give Death the slip, maybe—

MAN IN GREY
Come brother, a drink for our kinship's sake!

MAN IN MOURNING
Our kins be damned! You're a drunken rake!

MAN IN GREY
Blood is thicker than that, you old skin-flint!
One can't help feeling we're kin of Peer Gynt!
(Exit together)

PEER GYNT
(aside)
One meets old friends!

A LAD
(calling after Man in Mourning)
Have a care, Aslak, think!
Or mother will haunt you if you take a drink!

PEER
(getting up)
The farmer's wrong here, the deeper you shovel—
Say about six feet down—the sweeter the smell!

ASLAK
(with a bear-skin)
This is the pelt of the Dovrë-cat, they say,
That chased the Trolls out on Christmas Day!

ANOTHER
(with a pair of antlers)
And this is the buck Peer Gynt rode at dawn
Over Gendin Ridge and plunged into the tarn!

A THIRD
(calls out to Man in Mourning)
Aslak! Do you remember this hammer?
That cracked the nut that freed the evil bounder!

A FOURTH
(empty-handed)

Mads Möen, here's Peer's invisible cloak
In which he stole Ingrid from her kinsfolk!

PEER

I'm getting old, every second! Brandy, boys!
Come, I'll raffle off my Castles and my Toys!

A LAD

What have you got to sell, grandad?

PEER
A palace.

It's up at Rondë—quite a show-place!

THE LAD

I bid a penny!

PEER
And for a nip, yes—

'Twould be a sin to bid anything less!

ANOTHER LAD
(crowd gathers)

A jolly old gaffer!

PEER
My Blackie—my horse!

ONE OF THE CROWD

Where is he running now?

PEER
Why, out West, of course!

VOICES

What else have you got?

PEER
Both tinsel and gold,

I bought them with ruin—but the story is old!

A LAD

Put them up!

PEER

A dream of a prayer-book,
I'll let it go for—say a buttonhook!

THE LAD

The devil with dreams!

PEER

Here's my Kaiserdom,
I'll swap it for a jug of Jamaica rum!

THE LAD

How about your crown?

PEER

Near gold, without a flaw,
Made of the very finest Egyptian straw;
A monkey's tail, a madman's greying hair;
A Prophet's beard, a white Arabian mare;
They're yours—nothing like them in Norway,
Just show me the guidepost: This is the Way!

A CONSTABLE
(who has come up)

Oldtimer, that is quite enough for now,
Otherwise I'll have to take you to the hoosegow!

PEER
(hat in hand)

Very likely, but who was Peer Gynt, sir?

CONSTABLE

O nonsense!

PEER

I beg your indulgence, sir!

CONSTABLE

He was the most abominable liar, faker!

PEER

Faker?

CONSTABLE

Yes, he was a strange fellow,
He was an out-and-out tale-spinner,

Who always made out he was the Hero
Of each yarn. Excuse me, I must meet the Squire!
(Exit)

PEER

Where's he now, this remarkable tale-maker?

AN ELDERLY MAN

'Twas rumored years ago he was hung
For swindling rich mandarins of Hong Kong!

PEER

Hanged? Aye, aye, he was finally unmasked.
The late Peer Gynt was Himself to the last!
(Bows)

Good-bye!
(Goes a few steps, then stops)
Now, before you good folks adjourn,
I'd like to tell a story in return!

SEVERAL

Yes, do you know any?

PEER

Yes, as you will learn!
(Peer returns. A look of strangeness comes over him.)

I was once digging gold in San Francisco,
On the notorious Barbary Coast; the whole
Town was swarming with mountebank shows.
One man played a fiddle with his toes,
Another danced a Spanish fandango
On his knees, a third a Polish mazurka
On his hams, and a fourth naively composed
Verses while some quack calmly bored a hole
Through his head.

To this extravaganza
Came the Devil himself, incognito,
To try his luck with the rest of them. Dressed
In a cloak with a flying hood, he concealed
A small pig under his flowing mantle,
And said he could mystify the rabble

By imitating a pig. When he pinched
The pig it squealed or grunted. 'Twas a real
Fantasia and parody on a pig's life,
From birth to the dramatic slaughter-house squeal.

Then the connoisseurs debated, pro and con—
Some thought the tone entirely too thin,
Some the death scene seemed too genuine,
But they all agreed the whole goings-on,
Qua grunt, was grossly exaggerated;
In short, the Devil had miscalculated
In his haste, without reckoning the public's taste!
          (Bows out. A puzzled silence falls over the crowd.)

SCENE V

Whitsunday Eve. In the heart of the forest. In the back-
ground in a clearing, is a hut with a pair of antlers above the
door. Peer Gynt is seen groveling on all fours through the
undergrowth, grubbing for wild onions.

PEER GYNT

This is a quiet nook to orient oneself
And take inventory—I crave no pelf.
Sometimes second thoughts turn out the keenest.
Aye, prove all things and hold fast to the best.
I have done that—beginning with Caesar
And down as far as Nebuchadnezzar.
You see, I'm well versed in Bible history.
In course of time man returns to Mother Earth—
Ashes to ashes, dust to dust, and so forth!

The main thing in life is to fill your belly!
Fill it with onions? That's not so good!
If I had my old traps, I'd get better food.
And there's the brook, I won't suffer from thirst.

Of all the beasts, man always comes first!
We beasts, wild or tame, don't vary much, some talk
To be sure, but man's the only beast that can cook!

And when it comes time to shuffle off
I'll just crawl into some fallen tree-trough,
And like a bear, I'll pull the leaves over me;
Then I'll scrawl in big letters on the tree:
Here rests Peer Gynt, a famous Kaiser,
Who ate grass like Nebuchadnezzar!
Kaiser? Why you soothsaying rapscallion!
                    (Laughs to himself)
You're no Kaiser, you're only an onion!
I'm going to peel you now, my good Peer,
And I've a hunch you'll shed many a tear!
                    (Peeling an onion, layer by layer.)
Here's the outermost layer with a rip—
That's a drowning man clinging to a ship!
And this is the Passenger-layer, thin as paper,
Yet a smack of Peer Gynt seems to linger;
Now, we come to the old gold-digger himself—
The juice of the leek is gone, like himself.

This hard-grained leaf with coarse skin, I'd say,
Is the grizzled trapper from Hudson Bay;
The next one reminds me of a lost crown,
I'd call it straw-colored or burnished brown;
Here's that mummyologist, dry as dirt;
And this, fresh and juicy, has a Prophet's quirk—
It stinks, just like the Good Book says, of lies
That will bring tears to an honest man's eyes;
Pshaw! and this one that's so tightly rolled,
Is an old miser a-counting his gold;
The next looks smudged, no doubt my smugglers—
Another guess would be, parsons and niggers!
                    (Pulls off several layers.)
Who'd a thought a leek had so many swathings.
Now, where's the core?
                    (Pulls onion apart)
                    Poof! Nothing but peelings!

Nature is clever!

(Throws the bits away.)

The Devil take all thinking!
One's liable to stumble with such tinkering!
Anyhow, I can laugh at danger in the face,
To be meek, crawl on all fours, is no disgrace!

(Scratches back of his head.)

Life is a long gamble—sometimes a prize
For the beginner, and blanks for the wise!

(He nears the hut, looks at it, starts, rubs his eyes.)

That little hut in the grot looks familiar—
A pair of antlers above the cabin-door,
A mermaid like a fish from the navel,
A wooden gargoyle jutting from the gable.
Nonsense! Only log planks, an iron bolt,
And bars to give the goblins a jolt!

SOLVEIG

(Singing in the hut)

Tomorrow is Whitsunday.
Fifty years ago this eve,
He carried me through the door;
With a kiss he took his leave,
Silently over the moor.
Dearest lad of mine, some day
You will come across the moor,
And find me waitin' as of yore!

PEER

(Quiet and deadly pale)

One who remembers, and one who forgot,
One who prayed, and one who wandered!
My soul's afire! I feel like one redeemed!
God wot! My kingdom was here in this grot!

(Runs off into the woods.)

SCENE VI

*Night. A heath with fir trees. A forest fire has been raging,
and burning and charred tree stumps are seen for miles
around. Patches of white mist curl here and there from the
waste. Peer Gynt comes running over the heath.*

PEER GYNT
Ashes, fog and dust flying,
Enough here for building,
Where stench and rot gather,
A whitewashed sepulchre!
Let ken, dreams and dull wit
Lay my tomb, bit by bit;
Let Falsehood and her heirs
Build the winding stairs,
Fear instead of repentance,
Curses instead of remorse,
Judgment's trumpet perforce,
Shall sound the sentence!
When my eager eyes are closed,
And my body disposed,
Summon the good people,
And, high upon the steeple
On a golden shield, write:
Petrus Gyntus Caesar Fecit!

(Listens)

What have we here?
What grates my ear?
Children weeping,
Threadballs fluttering!
        (Kicking at them.)
Away! Stop your crying!

THE THREADBALLS
(on the ground)
We are only thoughts,
Don't you remember?
Like forget-me-nots,
We have no feet, sir!

PEER

(going roundabout)

Yes, I have given life to one—
He was my bandy-legged son!

THE THREADBALLS

We cannot rejoice,
We have, sir, no voice;
We spend the whole day
In sighs and dismay!

PEER

(stumbling)

Threadballs! You accursed devils!
You're worse than a thousand weevils!

WITHERED LEAVES

(flying before the wind.)

We are a watchword,
And you were our sword,
But by your own sloth,
The worm and the moth
Gnawed us to death
On every heath;
No blessed garlands
Ever came from our hands!

PEER

Your life has not been in vain, I'm sure—
Lie still, and, in time, you'll serve for manure!

A SIGHING IN THE AIR

We are the folk songs
Which you should have sung,
But with your tart tongue
We're humiliated!
We lay and waited!
Down deep in your heart
You have kept apart!
Now, you'll feel our smart—
You shall be poisoned!

PEER

Poison yourselves! Never mind the curse!
Rats! I have no time for sing-song verse!
            (Takes a short-cut)

DEWDROPS

(Dripping from the branches)
    We are unshed tears.
    Icicles pierce the heart
    Which we could have melted.
    Now rankles the dart
    In the breast sealed.
    The wound is healed—
    Thus ends all our fears!

PEER

I wept when I was one of the contestants
At a troll-party. How they warmed my pants!

BROKEN STRAWS

    Old rogue, hold your tongue!
    We're deeds left undone.
    Frustrated by Doubt,
    Crippled ere begun.
    Hail the Juggernaut!
    On Doomsday, mister,
    When we all gather
    To tell our story—
    For you we're sorry!

PEER

Poppycock! How can you condemn one
For things he has never done!

ASE'S VOICE

(in the offing)
    Whoa! What a driver! Whoa!
    You've overturned the sleigh,
    Thrown me into the snow,
    And you have lost your way!
    Where is your castle now?

Turn back, Peer, save our lives!
With the whip the Devil drives!

PEER

Away! The devil's sins follow me round!
Wherever I go, I must give him ground!
O let me rest my weary bones on yon mound!
(Runs off)

SCENE VII

Another part of the heath.

PEER GYNT
(Singing)

Yoho! The sexton and his hounds,
With measured steps he makes his rounds.
     Above, below, around,
     Echoes the solemn sound—
     God have mercy—poor soul,
     God bless his snow-white poll,
The night is cold, the way is foul,
Tu-whit, tu-whoo, bewails the horned owl.

*(The Button-moulder with a tool-chest and a casting ladle,
comes from a side path)*

BUTTON-MOULDER

Well met, Old Timer!

PEER

Good evening, sir!

BUTTON-MOULDER

Why the hurry? Are you going somewhere?

PEER

To a funeral—

BUTTON-MOULDER

So! My sight's very bad, sir.
By the way, is your name by any chance, Peer?

PEER

Peer Gynt, at your service!

BUTTON-MOULDER
That's what I call luck;
I've been hunting all day for the peacock!

PEER

What for—who are you?

BUTTON-MOULDER
Well, you see, it's this way,
I'm a moulder, and must pour you to-day.

PEER

Pour?

BUTTON-MOULDER
Yes, here in my ladle I'll melt you!

PEER

Melt me?

BUTTON-MOULDER
Here it is, neatly scoured, too;
Your grave is dug, your coffin is ready,
And we will soon have you lapped in clay;
My good man, I have my orders, without delay,
From the good Master to bring in your body!

PEER

Impossible! Just like that, without warning!

BUTTON-MOULDER
O, it's an old custom at a christening
Or burial to keep the day of the feast quiet—
You know—sort of a surprise party, brother!

PEER

Very true! I'm getting dizzy. I forget,
You are—

BUTTON-MOULDER
I told you, sir, a button-moulder!

PEER

I understand. Just another brain-child,

The customary run-around, Mister Moulder.
I deserve some consideration, I'm sure.
I'm not as bad as some people picture,
And I've done a lot of good, a bit wild
At times; at the worst, I'm only a backslider,
But certainly not a dyed-in-the-wool sinner!

BUTTON-MOULDER

But that is just the very point, brother,
In reality you're not a downright sinner,
So you are excused all the pangs of hell,
If you'll only step into my ladle.

PEER

Call it what you like, ladle or cauldron,
Spruce and swipes are still near beer, Mister Button.
Away, Satan!

BUTTON-MOULDER
                 O now you're getting rude!
You don't mean, perchance, I'm a cloven hoof?

PEER

On your way, sir, fox's claws or cloven hoof,
Whichever you like, you are getting crude!

BUTTON-MOULDER

My friend, you are making a grave error.
Now, to save time—we're both in a hurry
It seems—I will explain the whole affair.
You are no real sinner in the true sense
Of the word, only a backsliding bungler!

PEER

Now you are beginning to talk horse-sense,
I thought, my friend, you were off your noodle!

BUTTON-MOULDER

Patience! But to call you good, an angel—

PEER

No, I have never laid claim to that, sir.

BUTTON-MOULDER

Well, I'd say, something betwixt and between—
We seldom see sinners of grandiose style
Nowadays—the real sinner is more masculine
In his vigor, and harder to reconcile.

PEER

You're perfectly right—one must go berserk!

BUTTON-MOULDER

I know, you took lightly to sin like a Turk!

PEER

O no, I'm just a little mud-splashed!

BUTTON-MOULDER

Right, the cauldron's no place for a dauber!

PEER

In that case, I'll leave right now, Mister Moulder!

BUTTON-MOULDER

No, friend, I must melt you up as ordered!

PEER

Nonsense! What new tricks have been invented
Since I have been prospecting and traveling?

BUTTON-MOULDER

Why man, the custom's as old as creation,
And designed to maintain perfection,
In keeping everything up to a standard.
You've worked at the craft—any inward
Defect shows up later in the casting!
In that case, what would you do?

PEER

Throw it away!

BUTTON-MOULDER

Correct! Your old man was a wastrel, they say,
Reckless when he had anything to waste.
My good Master, however, never debased
The Craft, and that's why he is so well-to-do,

For he always conserved raw material,
And above all, very economical,
Never threw anything away as the Gynts do.
Sir, you were meant for a shining button
On the world's vest, but, alas, I reckon
You'll have to go back into the cauldron,
Into the scrap-pile, sir, much to my sorrow!

PEER

Do you mean I'll have to be melted down
With any Tom, Dick and Harry? I've grown
Accustomed to better things in my day.

BUTTON-MOULDER

Yes, that's what they do at the mint, they say,
When a coin is worn out or defective.

PEER

Man, the thought is distinctly offensive.
What's a loopless button, a worn-out coin,
To a great man of your Master's coign?
Now, if you don't mind, I'll say adieu!

BUTTON-MOULDER

As long as you've the right spirit in you
The good Master might allow you face value!

PEER

A thousand times no! The idea's absurd!

BUTTON-MOULDER

Calm down, friend, before you get tired!
Furthermore, you're even too light for Heaven!

PEER

I'm not hard to please, and I don't aim high,
But I won't forfeit one iota. Now, why
Not have me tried in the old-fashioned way,
Or better, parole me to the Devil, say
For a hundred years or so at the utmost.
Here the torture, my friend, is mostly moral,
And transitional. In time the prodigal
Returns, and lives in hope of better days;

But to melt me up in a ladle like keys,
Buttons, riff-raff, and every thingumagig
Stirs up my soul, and I vehemently renege!

BUTTON-MOULDER

Calm yourself, man, there's no need for a fuss,
You've never been yourself, so why rave and cuss,
You've got one foot in the grave now, old sourpuss!

PEER

Is that so! Ho-ho! You make me laugh, brother!
I'm Peer Gynt, out and out! I have no peer!
Take a look, Buttons, all you see is ME here!

BUTTON-MOULDER

Don't get on your high horse! Here's my warrant,
A requisition: "Deliver one Peer Gynt—
He's a misfit, spoilt, damaged goods. Re-mint."

PEER

Poppycock! Why do you act so arrogant?
You've confused me with John or Rasmus Gynt!

BUTTON-MOULDER

O no, friend. I melted them down long ago.
No, come along. I'll escort you to the mint!

PEER

No! I'll be damned if you do! Tomorrow
You'll discover you melted down the wrong man!
Sir, you've a responsibility—be human!

BUTTON-MOULDER

Sorry, I have my orders!

PEER

              Give me a respite!

BUTTON-MOULDER

What good will that do?

PEER

              I'll show you I'm right,
That I have always been myself all my life,
And this is the way to end all this strife.

BUTTON-MOULDER

Prove by what? I really don't comprehend!

PEER

I'll get bonafide testimonials, my friend!

BUTTON-MOULDER

They'll hardly satisfy my Master, I fear!

PEER

Just give me another day or so, my good sir,
Just loan me to myself, I'll return right soon.
We are born *once,* live *once,* and die ditto!
Come sir, are we agreed? Grant me this boon!

BUTTON-MOULDER

Very well, Mister Peer Gynt, do as you like;
But remember, we'll meet at the next turnpike!

(Exit)

SCENE VIII

Another part of the heath.

PEER GYNT
(running fast)

Time is money now. Where do the roads cross?
They may be far or just over yon knoll.
The earth beneath feels like a red-hot coal.
A witness! A witness! Where shall I find one?
Unlikely, here in the woods. The world's all dross
Where a right must be proved, that's plain as the sun!

*(An old man, bent with years, with a staff in hand and a sack
over his shoulder, trudges slowly in front of Peer Gynt.)*

THE OLD MAN
(stopping)

Kind sir, can you spare an old man a penny?

PEER

Excuse me, sir, I haven't a sou with me!

OLD MAN

Prince Peer! O, to think we would meet this way!

PEER

Who are you?

OLD MAN

I'm the old man from the Rondë!

PEER

No! Why, who would think—

OLD MAN

The King of the Dovrë!

PEER

The King of the Trolls, really?

OLD MAN

I was dethroned!

PEER

Ruined?

OLD MAN

Stripped of everything and famished!

PEER

(snapping his fingers)

What luck! A splendid witness for my side!

OLD MAN

You have aged, too. You look somewhat mortified!

PEER

Come, let bygones be bygones, and above all
No family jars. I was wild then, I recall!

OLD MAN

The Prince was young, and youth must be satisfied,
And you were wise in rejecting the bride—
Saved yourself a lot of grief and worry,
For she's gone to the bad!

PEER

You don't tell me!

OLD MAN

She has had such a deplorable life, they say,
She and Trond are now living together.

PEER

Which Trond?

OLD MAN
Of the Valfjeld.

PEER
Wellaway!
The same, I cut him out with the Saeter girls!

OLD MAN

My grandson has grown up to be a fine fellow,
With a flock of children in every borough!

PEER

But to come to the point, I need your aid.
I'm in a ticklish position and afraid
If I don't find a character witness soon,
I'm a doomed man!

OLD MAN
I'll grant you this boon,
Your Highness, if you'll do the same for me!

PEER

Gladly, but I'm hard pressed for ready money,
But, hear my story—you remember the night
I came to court the Princess?

OLD MAN
Quite right,
My Lord Prince!

PEER
Just skip the Prince stuff!
You tried to make me a Troll. That wasn't enough,
You wanted to snip my eyeball, to distort
My eyesight. Recall how I swore I'd stand
On my own feet, gave up love, power and land,
All, for the sake of being Myself again.
I want you to swear to these facts in court!

OLD MAN
O, I couldn't do that!

PEER
Such idle talk, man!

OLD MAN
Surely you don't want me to lie for you!
Even a poor beggar has some honor left!
You donned our Troll gear and drank our mead.

PEER
You know you didn't give me a square deal, instead
You hoodwinked me with promises, almost bereft
Me of my senses, and turned me out without a sou!

OLD MAN
Just the opposite, my son—

PEER
What do you mean?

OLD MAN
During the Rondë ceremonies you subscribed
To the Troll-creed!

PEER
What creed?

OLD MAN
Our sacred doctrine
The which that distinguishes a Troll from the rest
Of mankind: Troll, To Thyself Be Enough!

PEER
(recoiling)
Enough!

OLD MAN
Come now, Lord Prince, don't get excited,
You've been a Troll ever since, I can attest!

PEER
More idle talk, man!

OLD MAN
(weeping)
You're breaking my heart!
You've lived like a Troll from the very start,
Unconsciously, but now you thumb your nose
At the word that has been your inspiration,
Yes, your own salvation, everyone knows!

PEER

Enough! A Troll hill-billy! An upstart!
Impossible! Such nonsense, such distortion!

OLD MAN
(Pulling out a bundle of old newspapers)
Look at these, son. I read the newspapers,
I know all about you and your wild capers.
Now, I'll show you right here in black and red
How the "Bloksberg Post" praises you to the sky,
While the "Heklefjeld Journal" prints an all-high
Article from the East: Why the heathen Chinese darn
White hose with black thread and black with white yarn.
Why, the Chinese have been Trolls for centuries.
They do everything upside down like us pixies!
Here's one signed Stallionhoof, and a conceited
Paper on "Troll Nationalism"—all signed by our Peer!
"Our Enough," he says, "is Trolldom's gift to man!"
And cites and quotes us, again and again!

PEER

I? A hill-billy Troll?

OLD MAN
That's perfectly clear!

PEER

In that case I should have stayed in the Rondë
In peace and comfort, and spared myself trouble,
Grief and shoe-leather! A Troll! Mumbo-jumbo!
Good-bye, King Troll, here's a penny for tobacco!

OLD MAN

O no, my good Prince!

PEER

Stop this nonsense!
Away! You're in your dotage—in a trance!

OLD MAN

O, that's the most unkindest cut of all!
My descendants are very powerful throughout
The land, but alas, they insist I only exist
In hornbooks. They all say in-laws are, no doubt,
The most ungrateful people in the world,
And I hope the Lord charges them with my downfall!

PEER

You're not the only one the Maelstrom hurled—

OLD MAN

You know we Trolls have no Old Age Pension,
No Poor Box and no Postal Savings Bank—
Such things would be considered treason
In the Troll-kingdom!

PEER

All the work of some crank,
Including your confounded Troll-slogan—
To Thyself Be Enough!

OLD MAN

Why, my good man,
You have no cause to grumble, prosperity—

PEER

O, you're barking up the wrong tree, old Rex,
I am at the end of my rope!

OLD MAN

Impossible!
Your Highness ruined?

PEER

Yes, I'm one of your wrecks!
Just shows what comes from such bad company!

OLD MAN

Good-bye, Your Highness! All my hopes and ambitions

Are blasted! I'll go and see what's down town!

PEER
What would you do there that's praiseworthy?

OLD MAN
The theater! I can play anything from a clown
To the star role, and good actors are scarce!

PEER
Good Luck to you! I, too, have aspirations
For the stage. Some day I'll write a lusty farce
That will bring, I hope, fame and fortune to me;
I'll call it: Sic transit gloria mundi.

(Disappears in the copse, the Old Man calling after him.)

SCENE IX

PEER GYNT
(At a Cross-road)
Well, Old Man Gynt, here's the end of the line!
Now, you see what the Troll's "Enough" has done for you!
Your poor ship is a wreck—it has struck a mine!
O, grab a spar, quick, or you go down with the crew!

BUTTON-MOULDER
(At the cross-road)
Your testimonials, sir!

PEER
What! You, again?

BUTTON-MOULDER
I'm a mind reader! You're a dead duck, man!

PEER
I'm weary of running—I might lose my way!

BUTTON-MOULDER
You're right, but what does it lead to, after all?

                    PEER
Through the woods, into the night—

                    BUTTON-MOULDER
                         Eternity, I'd say.
There goes an old man—shall we call him here?

                    PEER
No, let him go; he's drunk, beyond recall!

                    BUTTON-MOULDER
He might perhaps—

                    PEER
                    Hush, let's forget him, sir!

                    BUTTON-MOULDER
Well, come along, then!

                    PEER
                    Just one more question!
What is "being oneself?"

                    BUTTON-MOULDER
                    I beg your pardon,
Did I hear aright?

                    PEER
                    No evasions, sir!

                    BUTTON-MOULDER
To be oneself is to slay the baser self,
But I deem the answer over your head;
In short, carry out daily the Master's creed!

                    PEER
Suppose I don't know—

                    BUTTON-MOULDER
                    Follow your conscience!

                    PEER
O, you mean the still small voice, perchance—

                    BUTTON-MOULDER
There's no hell like a bad conscience, my friend—
One devil's as bad as another, I contend!

PEER

Now, we're getting into deep water. I plead
Guilty of not being myself. As I wandered
Alone across the moor, I said o'er and o'er
To myself: After all, Peer, you're a sinner—

BUTTON-MOULDER

Now, now, man, we're right back where we started—

PEER

By no means—I mean a *great* one, not in deed
Only, but in thought and desire. I lived
A most detestable and vile life abroad!

BUTTON-MOULDER

Perhaps. Right now all I've got is your word.
Prove it!

PEER

Give me time to find a parson.
I'll get it down in black and white, Mister Button!

BUTTON-MOULDER

Do that now—it will clear things up greatly,
And you may yet escape the casting ladle!
You've seen my papers—

PEER

Yes, they're old and musty—
They go way back when I was a young rake,
Sold niggers, played prophet, and trusted to Fate!
I'll see you later.—

BUTTON-MOULDER

But—

PEER

My good man, take it easy.
I can see you have nothing to do here
In the parish. So invigorating's the air,
Many live to be as old as Methuselah!
A famous preacher once said: "It's very rare
That anybody ever dies in this valley!"

BUTTON-MOULDER

At the cross-road, Peer!

PEER

I'll be ready!

(Runs off)

SCENE X

A hill-side path.

PEER GYNT

Who would have thought a man's sins, in the end,
Would prove his own redemption, and extend
A helping hand? Yes or no, the whole affair
Is a riddle—it's out of the frying pan
Into the fire—just a jump ahead of Satan!
Ah well, as long as there's life there's hope, Peer!

*(A Thin Man in a priest's cassock, with a fowling net over
his shoulder, comes running down the path.)*

Who goes there? A parson with a fowling net!
Hurrah! My luck still holds up! Well met!
The path is very rough, sir; watch your step!

THE THIN MAN

Ah, yes, but what wouldn't one do for a soul!

PEER

O ho! then there's someone bound for heaven, sir?

THIN MAN

O no! I hope he has chosen the other goal!

PEER

May I walk with you part of the way?

THIN MAN

Gladly. I'm going down to the valley.

PEER

I have something on my mind—

THIN MAN

Speak up, brother!

PEER

You see before you, parson, an honest man.
I have always lived within the law; what's more
I've never been in jail, but now and then a man
Will miss his footing and stumble, I'm sure—

THIN MAN

That happens to the best of us—

PEER

These trifles, you see—

THIN MAN

Only trifles?

PEER

I've never done, believe me,
Any wholesale sinning—

THIN MAN

I'm not interested.
I'm not the man you think. Why are you looking
At my fingers? What do you see in them?

PEER

Your nails are remarkably developed.

THIN MAN

And now at my feet you are gazing!

PEER
(pointing)

A natural hoof?

THIN MAN

Very normal, I gather.

PEER
(doffing his hat)

I would have sworn you are only a pastor,

So I have the honor—well, don't forget that
When the front door's open, avoid the kitchen door,
When you meet the King, avoid the Royal Door Mat!

THIN MAN

Shake! You seem to be free from prejudice!
Now, in what way may I be of service?
But don't ask me, sir, for power or gold;
However, I'll do the best I can, I promise.
Lately business has slumped a hundredfold,
Maybe only a stray soul now and then.

PEER

You mean to say the world's getting better?

THIN MAN

O no! Just the reverse—most of the brethren
End up in the casting-ladle, sooner or later.

PEER

Ah yes, I've heard much about that ladle
From a friend, and now I seek your advice.

THIN MAN

Speak up, sir!

PEER

Well, if it's not too much trouble,
I would like—

THIN MAN

A place of refuge, I surmise.

PEER

That's it, sir; you admit business is poor,
And I thought you might leave open the door—

THIN MAN

But—

PEER

My demands are very reasonable,
I seek no wages, only a cozy ingle—

THIN MAN

A nice warm room?

PEER

But not too hot; I prefer
To go and come at will, should something better
Turn up later—

THIN MAN

I am extremely sorry,
But you can't imagine how many requests
Of the same nature I receive from guests
Leaving the scene of their earthly activity.

PEER

My dear friend, when I think of my past career,
I feel that I'm a qualified candidate—

THIN MAN

Mere trifles, you said—

PEER

In a general way, I swear,
Though I sold slaves—

THIN MAN

Yes, the bunglers still cheat.
Even lame ducks are refused entry.

PEER

And I shipped heathen idols to China.

THIN MAN

More wish-wash. We have savants, I dare say,
Who traffic in souls, literature and art,
But who can't get in.

PEER

Then, too, I was once a prophet.

THIN MAN

Poof! All con-men end up in the casting ladle,
And I write the epitaph for the riff-raff!
No, you'll have to do better than that, uncle!

PEER

Once I could have saved a cook from the foam,
Then I remembered "Charity begins at home,"
And his drowning was due to my loss of heart.

THIN MAN

In times like this I cannot waste good coal.
As a sinner you're a tyro, out and out.
What would you gain if I gave you lodging
And board? You have no cause for rejoicing,
Neither have you anything to worry about,
So I say, Be a good sport, resign your soul
To the casting ladle as all sinners do.

PEER

But it's only the wearer of the shoe
Who can tell where the shoe is pinching.

THIN MAN

Speaking of shoes, that reminds me, I must go
And burnish a *bonne bouche* on the spit.

PEER

Your sin-diet must be very exquisite.

THIN MAN

Nevertheless, he is Himself, my friend.

PEER

You have sinners like that? You condescend—

THIN MAN

Now, take this negative of an old photo
I have here; for years it's laid in my *bordereau*,
Frightfully corroded, you can see, by brimstone,
But by cosmic art I restore the unknown
And the forsaken, as in your own case.

PEER

Who is he? You cannot tell by that face!

THIN MAN

One Peer Gynt—Sir Peter, the records show.

PEER

No foolin'! Is he still Himself, and alive?

THIN MAN

Yes, he thinks he is—

PEER

An honest man, I believe?

THIN MAN

Did you know him?

PEER

I knew his grandfather.

THIN MAN

I must be going. Have you seen him lately?

PEER

At the Cape—

THIN MAN

Of Good Hope?

PEER

Yes, he's about ready

To sail again—

THIN MAN

I must leave without delay,

I only hope I run into him on the way,
And the Cape's flooded with converts from Stavanger.
(He rushes off)

PEER

Poof! He's off on my trail like a bloodhound!
The silly ass, he's just another stuffed shirt!
Every unfortunate sinner he can't convert,
He consigns the poor soul to the dog-pound!
It's a feather in my hat to pull the wool
Over a hypocrite like that. There's no fool
Like an old fool. My own position, however,
Is precarious—I've been disowned by the Trolls
And lost Myself! I can feel the ladle's hot coals!
(Waves at a falling star)

Greetings Brother Star from Brother Peter!
Another poor soul kicked out of heaven;

(Pulling himself together he plunges deeper into the mist.)

Is there no one, no one in this lonely glen,
No one in this abyss, no one in heaven—

*(Comes out farther down, throws his hat on the ground, and
    tears his hair. Slowly a stillness comes over him.)*

Impossible! Can a soul so miserably poor
Return into the mist and become nothing?
Beautiful Earth, forgive my trespassing!
Beautiful Sun, thou hast squandered thy beams
On empty walls—there never was anyone
At home to cheer, to warm, or to nurture.
O Beautiful Sun, O Beautiful Earth,
You were foolish to succor my mother at birth.
The spirit's niggard, Nature's a spendthrift it seems—
A life for one's birth is a dear price to pay.
Up to the highest mountain peak I will go,
Once more I will look on the rising sun,
And gaze upon the Promised Land all day,
And at even, like all sinners, I'll fade away!
For my epitaph write: "Here Lies No One."

CHURCH FOLK
(Singing on their way to worship)

Awake! 'Tis Whitsunday morn,
Praise Him with timbrel and horn,
        Extol His name!
The lightning's flash in the clouds,
The resounding roll of chords,
        Proclaim His fame.

PEER
(crouching in fear)

Come, Trolls, sew me up in my pigskin,
And bury me behind my cabin!

(Creeps into the bushes but comes up on the crossroad.)

SCENE XI

At a cross-road.

BUTTON-MOULDER
Good Morning, Peer Gynt! Did you bring your list?

PEER GYNT
I have shouted and run myself ragged!

BUTTON-MOULDER
You found no one?

PEER
Only a confounded atheist!

BUTTON-MOULDER
Then you are a dead duck!

PEER
Everything's pixilated,
And the moping owl bids the moon good-bye!

BUTTON-MOULDER
That's the matins bell—

PEER
(pointing)
What's that light, so nearby?

BUTTON-MOULDER
A light from yon hut!

PEER
And that wailing sound?

BUTTON-MOULDER
Only a woman singing—

PEER
My list has been found!

BUTTON-MOULDER
(seizes him)
Come, Peer Gynt, put your house in order!

(They have come out of the woods and are standing in front
of the hut. Daybreak.)

· PEER

Be gone! That's it! I'll put my house in order!
Away! Were your ladle as big as two coffins,
It would not hold me and my list of sins!

BUTTON-MOULDER

Well, to the third cross-road, then beware!

PEER
(approaches the hut)

Backward or forward, it is just as far,
In or out, the way is just as narrow.
I seem to hear a voice, so soft and low—
Come home, come in my boy, forget your pride,
Let the light in the window be your guide!

(Takes a few steps then stops. Hears singing in the hut.)

Go roundabout, said the Boyg! Let no one gainsay
This time, I didn't take the straight and narrow way.

(He runs towards the hut, and at the same time Solveig is
seen in the doorway, dressed for church, with a prayer-book
wrapped in a kerchief, and a staff in her hand.)

(Peer throws himself down on the threshold)

Hast thou doom for a sinner? Then speak the word!

SOLVEIG

Peer! Peer, my lad! O praised be the Lord!
(Groping for him)

PEER

Cry out all the sins I have committed!

SOLVEIG

O my own lad, in naught hast thou sinned!
(Again groping, finds him)

BUTTON-MOULDER
(From behind the hut)

Your sin-list, Peer Gynt!

PEER

Call out my sins, loud and strong!

SOLVEIG

(Sitting down beside him.)

Thou has made my life a beautiful song,
Blest, blest be thou, my lad, who was lost
And thrice blest this morn of the Pentecost!

PEER

Then I am lost!

SOLVEIG

Turn to Him when in trouble—

PEER

(with a laugh)

I am lost, unless you can solve this riddle!

SOLVEIG

What is it, lad?

PEER

Where have I been, O my soul!

SOLVEIG

Been?

PEER

Fettered with Destiny's iron chain,
Been, with the image of God in my brain;
Tell me, lass, or I'll go the way of Cain!

SOLVEIG

The riddle's solved!

PEER

Tell me, where was the real Peer,
With the mark of Fate and God upon his soul?

SOLVEIG

In my faith, in my hope and in my love!

PEER

(starts back)

What are you saying? Will you swear to Him above
That you are the mother to the man that's there?

SOLVEIG

Yes, that I am, but who is his father?
Surely, he who forgives at a mother's prayer!

PEER

(His face beams, and he cries out)

My mother, my wife—thou innocent woman!
Forgive me—no greater love hath any man!

(Clings to her and buries his face in her lap. Sunrise.)

SOLVEIG

(singing softly)

I'll rock you to sleep, darling;
All day long he's been playing,
Sleep and dream, lad.

All is peaceful, all is still,
Save the hunter on the hill,
And the blackbird in the rill,
Sleep and dream, lad.

While rosy morn is creeping,
Softly the matins stealing,
I my vigil am keeping,
Sleep and dream, lad.

BUTTON-MOULDER

(from behind the hut)

At the next cross-road, Peer, we'll meet again;
I'll say no more, but see you keep your bargain!

SOLVEIG

(singing louder)

I'll rock you to sleep, darling;
All day long he's been playing,
Sleep and dream, lad!

(Curtain)